154 Pr.

TURTLE AT MR HUMBLE'S

A family of the 1790s, from an oil painting by
William Owen.

Turtle at Mr Humble's

The fortunes of a mercantile family
England & America 1758-1837

Pamela Rae

First published in 1992 by

Smith Settle Ltd
Ilkley Road
Otley
West Yorkshire
LS21 3JP

Text and selection of excerpts
© Pamela Rae 1992

The Whittaker Papers are held by
Bradford District Archives, Bradford, West Yorkshire.

ISBN Paperback 1 870071 95 6
Hardback 1 870071 96 4

British Library Cataloguing-in-Publication Data:
A catalogue record is available for this book
from the British Library.

Designed, printed and bound by
SMITH SETTLE
Ilkley Road, Otley, West Yorkshire LS21 3JP

Contents

Acknowledgments

I have been greatly helped in this project by the expert advice and assistance of library, museum and archives staff. My special thanks are due to David James, Bradford District Archivist of the West Yorkshire Archives Service, for first drawing my attention to the Whittaker Papers and for his help to a novice researcher. I am also grateful to Lorraine Mackenzie, whose original catalogue of the papers was invaluable; to Elvira Wilmott, specialist librarian, local studies, Bradford Central Library; John Goodchild, principal local studies officer and archivist, Wakefield Libraries; and Gordon Watson, Wakefield Museum. I wish to thank M T Wright, Science Museum, South Kensington, London, for the information on the Chronoscope. I also owe thanks to Avril Hart, Victoria and Albert Museum, London; C Anne Wilson, Brotherton Library, Leeds; Peter Brears, director of museums, Leeds; M G Barford, City of Bradford Metropolitan Council; the staff of Manchester Central Library; Dr Alan Scarth of the Merseyside Maritime Museum; Kay Parrott of Liverpool Library; Stephen Hoffius and the staff of the South Carolina Historical Society; Kathryn Gaillard of the Charleston Museum; and Nelson and Suzee Boice, Steven Rae, John Thornton and Frances Honour, who have all helped me with points of information and advice.

I should like to thank the University of South Carolina Press for permission to quote the comments of François Michaux and Governor Drayton from their publication *South Carolina: The Grand Tour*, and the South Carolina Historical Society for permission to quote from *The Letters of Charles*

Caleb Cotton (*South Carolina Historical and Geneaological Magazine*, July 1950), and *George Washington's Journal*, as quoted in *Charleston: Crossroads of History* by Isabella G Leland. The information on Charleston epidemics is largely taken from an article 'Stranger's Fever' by M Foster Farley (*South Carolina History Illustrated*, February 1970), also owned by the South Carolina Historical Society. I am grateful to Elvira Wilmott and Bradford Libraries for permission to quote from *The Diary of Dr John Simpson*, and the University of Leeds for permission to quote from an article by W G Briggs in their *Institute of Education Researches and Studies*, No 15, 1957 on 'Richmal Mangnall and her school at Crofton'.

In trying to unravel the business history of the period I have found invaluable *The Defence of British Trade 1689-1815* by Patrick Crowhurst and *The Growth of the British Cotton Trade 1780-1815*, by Michael M Edwards, and acknowledge my debt to these two authors.

I am grateful to Smith Settle Ltd for their encouragement in the project and Mark Whitley for his editorial guidance. Finally, I owe the greatest debt to my husband, Ian Rae, for his excellent judgment on all points.

Illustrative Acknowledgments

Thanks are due to the following for permission to reproduce pictures:

Board of Trustees of the National Museums and Galleries on Merseyside, p79; Board of Trustees of the V&A, pp23, 55, 60; Bradford Art Galleries and Museums, p211; Bradford Libraries, p223; Christies Colour Library, frontispiece; Historic New Orleans Collection Museum/Research Center (acc no 1974.25.13.271), p111; Leeds Reference Library, pp2, 4; Lincolns Inn Library, p125; Liverpool Libraries, p78; Manchester Public Libraries, pp49, 50, 94; National Maritime Museum, London, p99; Naval Historical Centre, Washington DC, pp106, 176; South Carolina Historical Society, p86; Walker-Neesam Archive, p10; West Yorkshire Archive Service, pp25, 40, 59, 66, 89, 119.

Ted Gower provided the specially-commissioned sketches on pages 19, 20, 21, 28, 85, 88 and 103.

The remainder of the illustrations are from the author's own collection.

Introduction

I first became interested in Sarah Whittaker and her family by accident, when I chanced on an article written by David James, the district archivist for Bradford, West Yorkshire. In it he described some of the archive collections in his care waiting for the attention of historians.

Among them, he wrote alluringly, was a collection of 'sparkling eighteenth century letters' – the Whittaker Papers. Hooked like a fish by this bait, I made an appointment to see them. In the Bradford archives reading room I began to take the letters out of their strong manilla envelopes and found no fewer than 166 items, some up to ten pages long, dating from 1758 to 1836. They were a daunting prospect, and, as a journalist, not a professional historian, I had not really given any thought to the realities of yellowing paper, fading ink and difficult handwriting.

I read one of Sarah Whittaker's own letters first, however, and quickly decided I should have to persevere in unravelling her story. Her fun-loving and lively personality seemed to jump off the page, her voice speaking as directly as if she were writing today.

She was born Sarah Buck in 1760, and died in 1837. Her life began in wealth and comfort in leisurely Georgian Bradford, which was then a small manufacturing town. The manuscripts were a family collection, written by Sarah, her husband, brother, parents and other relatives. Their handwriting, if often difficult, was at least varied, and the different personalities of the writers soon began to stand out clearly.

Sarah's handwriting was fluent, intelligent and relatively

easy to read, as was the careful, but graceful, business-trained script of her husband William. Her half-brother John's impatient scrawl was inclined to give me spots before the eyes, and her Aunt Todd's painfully elaborate scratchings revealed her anxious and affectionate soul. Uncle Stephen Todd's commanding, no-nonsense masculine hand was very legible, as was the exceptionally attractive writing of John Buck, Sarah's father, and the old-fashioned but readable hand of her mother Jenny. Business letters, written in a clerk's script, were as clear as a bell.

It soon became obvious that many of the letters preserved in the collection were careful copies of important communications. Without the help of typewriter or carbon paper, correspondents had to make their own written copies for reference, and also often made notes for their letters before finally putting pen to paper. John William Buck, Sarah's half-brother, who was a London barrister, asks his sister to make a fair copy, 'properly stopped and large Lettered', of a letter he wanted her to read before posting it on.

Their high-quality rag paper was expensive and seldom wasted. The backs of the letters were often used by the recipients for notes and calculations on other matters. Writing with scratchy quill pens dipped in the inkwell, often by the dim light of a candle or oil lamp, the letter-writers of two hundred years ago took great pains with their 'epistles', and their efforts were designed to last.

Letters were folded into three and sealed, with the address written on the outside. There was no envelope. They were charged by the sheet and weight, plus the distance, and most significantly, the recipient had to pay the charge, not the sender. This could cause some irritation – Sarah once complained that her daughter wrote on too thick paper, clumsily folded, which meant that the letter 'was charged double'. It was not until 1840 that the idea of a national cheap letter rate, with prepaid stamps – the famous 'penny post' – was introduced.

The postal system had developed by the eighteenth century

into a reasonably efficient service, with relay stations or 'posts' along the main routes radiating from London. Postboys on horseback carried the mail until they were superseded by the stagecoach, and later, by the faster, light mailcoach. Local carriers were also allowed to serve areas not covered by the government network.

One curious feature of my lengthy study of the letters was that when I first began to decipher Sarah's own letters, they seemed to have a quaintly 'period' flavour. But after I had read her mother's letters and become attuned to the time-warp of the '1760s set', Sarah's letters of the 1790s put on a modern air. She wrote differently, with a racy humour and directness which contrasts with the old-fashioned formality of her mother, her father and her Uncle and Aunt Todd. She was an up-to-the-minute young wife of the '1790s set', and that is how I think of her now.

Although occasionally the sentences fall over themselves and lose the network of syntax, on the whole the writers expressed themselves in elegant and sinewy English with a wide and varied vocabulary. My own grammar received a salutary jolt by reading these formal yet lively compositions. They are often a very high expression of 'the Epistoliary Art', to quote the forlorn Aunt Todd's characteristically-spelt phrase. Punctuation and spelling were both less formalised than today, and especially in the earlier years there is a tendency to give every important word a capital letter. I have not attempted to alter the spelling or style of expression to modern usage. Ellipses (. . .) are used to denote omitted words, and square brackets [ ] enclose explanatory points. Words or phrases underlined for emphasis in the letters are printed in italics.

Letter-writing was an art which kept social, business and family wheels turning, and provided a vital news service. 'Pray write soon', 'please write to your brother', 'how great my disappointment at not meeting with a single letter on my arrival', are recurring pleas for news.

A woman of Sarah's calibre was as capable of writing

good letters as her father, brother and husband. She held her own with her Cambridge-educated lawyer brother John, whose literary references clearly fell upon appreciative ears. Although officially women were not expected to engage in business, Sarah applied herself energetically to her husband's business problems. She was forced to use 'women's wiles', but she was shrewd in her understanding of commercial matters.

My first attempts to locate Townhill, the home of the Buck family, were something of a disaster. Well-meaning librarians sent me wandering round the windy hilltop village of Idle near Bradford on a wild goose chase, vainly quizzing bemused corner-shop grocers and local historians. It was not until I got back to the library, and was poring over a glass case displaying a large map of Bradford in the 1850s, that the name 'Townhill' leaped out at me in a totally unexpected spot. The house, a substantial mansion, had stood near the tollbooth at the start of the Wakefield road, just at the end of the old street of Goodmansend which led south from the centre of the town.

From that moment, the story of the family began to come clear, although I had many a struggle to come in disentangling the people and working out their relationships to each other. If modern days are distinguished by serial marriages and complicated relationships between half-brothers and sisters, in the eighteenth century it was death and remarriage, not divorce, which caused the confusion. There was also a trying tendency to give successive generations the same Christian names. Some pieces of the jigsaw were inevitably missing, and I have filled the gaps to the best of my deductive powers.

The letters do show clearly the cool and somewhat disdainful attitude the younger members of the family had for 'the Bradfordians', by whom they meant the new men of the mills who did not have their background or education. The Bucks identified more with the old families of the aristocratic network than with the industrial magnates of the future.

One 'need not idolize trade' to make a good career, says Sarah's brother, young John Buck, the university man, in typically haughty fashion. The Bucks and Whittakers were strictly of the comfortable merchant class, and their letters do not comment on the plight of hand weavers and spinners, starving or forced into badly-paid mill work – although desperate people stole food from their kitchens. There is only a sidelong view of the tremendous events of the French Revolution, the rise of Napoleon and the outbreak of the war with France. We read merely that young John Buck is glad he need not join the Volunteers now the threat of invasion is over, and that Sarah admired Bonaparte, even as late as 1815.

The business people in the story were acutely affected by the war, however, with its dislocation of trade and problems of communication. Ironically, it was the periodic outbreaks of peace which caused them the maximum confusion and difficulty . . .

Pamela Rae
1992

Prologue

In 1836 Sarah Whittaker, seventy-six years old, sitting in her house at Castle Park, Lancaster, took all the family letters out of the leather trunk in which long ago she had kept her jewels and gowns. She read them through slowly, once more.

'These letters are interesting to me', she wrote on the back of one of them, 'but when I am gone had better be burnt, unless Wm and Sarah [her children] wd like to look them over'.

It is not hard to imagine her sitting at her writing table, wearing her tortoiseshell spectacles ('Dolland's Grand Clearers') and trying to put the jumble of letters in order, frowning over some of them in annoyance.

'I often regret the hasty way I used to compose letters in the old days, without the proper heading', we can hear her say. 'But of course, when we were young, my dear husband William loved what he called my "enlivening scrawls". Naturally we knew what year it was at the time. But now it irritates me vastly to see how I used to write simply – "Sunday morning, Townhill".

All of us in the family have complained at times about each other's careless penmanship. How anyone ever managed to read my brother John's professional opinions I cannot imagine, although he was a most successful barrister. My husband William used to call John's handwriting his "scratching".

I fear that even if my children ever make the effort to read this trunkful of letters, they may have some difficulty in deciphering them. They themselves are not guiltless of scribbling – especially my daughter Sarah. When my son William was a student he used to say that his sister's letters sent him to "the kingdom of Puzzledom".

Some of my mother's letters date from before her marriage in 1759, which makes them nearly eighty years old. I find it very interesting to read letters written long before our great wars with Bonaparte. Things are so different now. My parents would scarcely have enjoyed the rush of modern living, and it is not to my taste either.

I cannot imagine what my father John Buck would have made of Bradford today, now it is so dirty and crowded with mills and those rabbit warrens of houses. I must say that I felt some indignation with Dixon the builder, when I realised the kind of poky little terraces of houses, each scarcely fit for a couple of pigs, which he intended to erect on our dear green fields.

But my son William, who is very grave now he has taken the cloth, has explained to me, as did all my Bradford friends, that the old days are gone and there is no stopping progress. The new mill masters think only of making money. To do that they have to employ more and more men, and must find somewhere, however cramped, for them to live.

I cannot say I regard these terraces as "progress", and I hope they prove only temporary accommodation for the mill-workers. Surely people need more light and air to live comfortably.

My letters contain so many painful secrets that perhaps I ought to burn them, but somehow I cannot bring myself to do it. I tell myself that I am really keeping them for my children's sake, but I know, if I am honest, that that is not true. I keep them for myself; when I read them I can see my own life so clearly as it stretches back through the years. And I can see even further back into the past, to a time before the marriage of my parents, when my mother was a lively young girl . . .'

as good a Chance of Happiness as Most

Jenny and John, 1758-1766

Sarah Buck was born in 1760 into a family of well-to-do Bradford entrepreneurs. Her mother was Jenny (Jane) Dawson, the youngest daughter of a prosperous Leeds merchant, Samuel Dawson. Jenny was the youngest of four sisters. Her family lived at Wither, a substantial country establishment in Armley, Leeds, on the opposite bank of the River Aire from the ruins of Kirkstall Abbey. Samuel Dawson was a considerable property owner in the Leeds district.

Jenny's three sisters were comfortably married, Martha to Freeman Flower of Gainsborough and London, Margaret to Stephen Todd of London, and Sarah to Edward Humble, a Newcastle merchant. As often happens with a close-knit family of sisters, they frequently consulted and visited each other.

In 1758, a year before her marriage, Jenny Dawson was a high-spirited, fun-loving young woman with a wicked sense of humour. The letters she wrote are the earliest in the Whittaker collection.

She sat down in the summer of 1758 to write a letter to her friend Miss Gracy Marshall, who was visiting Malton. Carefully schooled in the etiquette of letter-writing by her governess, Jenny began:

> To Miss Marshall at Malton – My Dr Girl's favour I Recd for which Accept My Gratefull Thanks – Need I Say I Rejoiced to hear your Journey was Prosperous May Every Scene of life My Dr freind [*sic*] engages in be

1

A south-east prospect of Leeds in 1745.

Equally So and your happiness large as my Extended Wishes and lasting as your hopes –

With politeness catered for, Jenny continued with more interesting subjects. Gracy and her companion Miss Spurman had apparently enjoyed the kind of encounter for which young ladies wished ardently when travelling. But, it seemed, Gracy's courage had failed:

> I think Myself Much Obliged to you for Relating So Minutely the Particulars of your Journey – how could you Gracy refuse to So Agreeable a Youth at York the Grant of One Request Upon My Word I think you did Miss Spurman a great Compliment in giving her the Preference – I hope she Acknowledgd the favour . . . I Insist upon it you bring home a Spark with you – that is I mean Lead Him Captive in Your Chains –

'Sparks' and beaux were certainly the girls' main preoccupation, and the hunt for a husband often had a faintly

2

desperate ring to it. If young women failed to marry, their prospects were exceedingly depressing. Without work and with their inheritance tied up in trusts, they could never become free of the family or lead independent lives.

Jenny's spirits were high, however, as she entertained Miss Marshall with news of the latest likely prospect, who had reappeared in Leeds after polishing his manners in London:

Must Not Forget to insert my favourite Youth for whom Every Heart Must Glow with Admiration is now at Leeds – How can I or any of My Sex view with Indifference so many Virtues conspicuous to every beholder Nor is it Possible to Conceal the Shining Excellences of his Character Any More than the Beauties of his person which Must Attract the Female World –

After this Encomium it Will Be Needless to tell you I mean Mr Winn Just Arrived Sparkling new from London – he had Charms Surpassing half his Sex before he went to that great Metropolis, and thinks now it Must Be impossible for Any to See Him And Live – I have not had that Pleasure yet but Intend Setting my Cap at him Tomorrow at Church – I am in great Spirits I Assure you and Nothing could So Well Reconcile me to Your Absence as This Fortunate Event of having Him All to Myself Possession is a great deal Gracy, and you are Far Enough Absent – If you Write to me soon in my next I will Give You an Account of his Behaviour to me which I Dare Say will be Particular Enough So Much for Beau Winn –

I have Never been at Leeds and can Give you Nothing of What is Done There – Except I could learn the Language of the Featherd Songsters and Entertain my Freinds with a Prospect of a Gothic Abbey and the murmuring of a Rivulet – but will not Attempt It lest you think Me Romantick – and to be Honest a Different Subject Occupies my Thoughts –

3

Jenny had been brought up at a time when good sense and a sharply unsentimental view of life were mandatory in polite society. The word 'Romantick' at that time meant everything to which civilised people were opposed – extravagance of action and mood, self-searching, an excessively emotional and affected preference for nature and wild scenery. 'Gothic' was a fashionable term for the ancient and mysterious past, whose ruins awoke the imagination. The view from Jenny's home of the opposite bank of the River Aire certainly included the 'Prospect of a Gothic Abbey' – the tumbling stones and broken arches of ruined Kirkstall.

As it happened, Mr Winn had no real chance of Jenny's attention, for the 'Different Subject' which occupied her thoughts was a serious one. A new dimension had recently been added to her flirtations:

Gracy, you Ask Me the Particulars of my Amour with Altamont which for the future shall be his Name. Indeed I am At a Loss what to Answer – I Can Only Say that his Visits are continued nor has my Freinds As Yet Advanced Any Material Objections – I told him it was

The ruins of Kirkstall Abbey.

my Fixd Resolve that I woud be free from Any
Engagement till July . . . Have took some pains Gracy
to Inform Myself of his Character and hear Nothing but
what is greatly in his favour – Notwithstanding all this
my freind I have a Thousand Doubts in My Own Breast
and Am a Strange Compound of hope and fear I think
if I had Matrimony in a Near View I should be Strangely
Frightened – Though from his General Character I
Believe I should Have as good a Chance of Happiness
as Most who Enter that State . . . Keep this Secret
within Your Own Breast and Pray in Return for the
Confidence Reposd in you tell me what success you
have had at Malton – Accept Dr Girl the True Esteem
of your Sincere freind, J. Dawson
          P.S. Burn this as Soon as read I Entreat you

The mysterious and incognito 'Altamont', the object of
such anxious ponderings, was undoubtedly her future
husband, John Buck, though what a down-to-earth Bradford
wool man made of his sweetheart's literary vapourings is not
recorded.

Forthcoming marriage into this sober and sensible family
of Bradford woolstaplers concentrated Jenny's mind wonderfully. The saucy secrets of beaux and sparks were forgotten
in November 1758, when she adopted a solemn and
improving tone to her young niece Lidia ('Miss Flower,
Gainsborough'). Perhaps she wrote with a sly smile – who
knows?:

My Dear Girl's Obliging Epistle was Recd. with True
Pleasure for which she has My Sincerest Thanks – the
Affectionate Manner in which My Dear Lidia expressd
her high Obligations to the Best of Parents gave me
Great Satisfaction . . . I think Myself much Obligd for
Your Strict Observance of the Little Rules I Requested
in your Pocket Book – Was glad to find by Yours to
Aunt Peggy that My Dear Girl was a Sharer in the
Entertainments for the King's Birthday, and the Con-

clusion I drew from it was that by her Diligence and Industry she had made some Considerable Improvement in Learning, and that her Mama, always Studious to Reward Merit, had granted the Kind Indulgence

Your Papa writes us you are to be a Performer at the next Ball, and Doubt not that Mr Cook will gain Great Credit from his young Scholar.

John Buck and Jenny Dawson were married in 1759. He settled on his wife 'all that estate at Goodmansend where my father now dwells along with £1000 in cash'. At the start of their married life the young couple probably lived in the family house next to their business premises. Sarah Buck, their only child, was born in 1760.

The Bucks' business was wool, and their house looked down across the pleasant meadows or 'ings' and Bradford Beck towards the parish church. In the valley where the beck flowed there was also a green called the Turls, where the people played bowls or the local game of knur and spell. There were just over 4,000 inhabitants in the little town. The

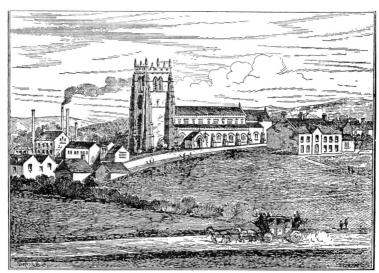

Bradford

6

valley was thickly wooded and the town nestled, almost hidden, among the trees. The Buck family and their friends enjoyed walking and riding in the woods, and the other pleasures of country living.

The church had become famous during the Civil War when the inhabitants of Bradford 'sandbagged' its tower with fleeces to protect it from the guns of the besieging Royalist forces. Dead Lane, which led from the parish church towards Goodmansend where the Bucks lived, received its grisly name from the corpses which are said to have been piled up there after the battle.

John's father, Joseph Buck, was one of the substantial woolstaplers who were key figures in the textile world of Yorkshire at this period. He came from Allerton-cum-Wilsden, a village to the west of Bradford, and by 1748 he already had a comfortable property at Goodmansend on the south side of Bradford. He leased this for the 'rent of One Red Rose' to his son John, who became his partner in the family business.

Mid-eighteenth century woolstaplers were men of capital and business ability. They organised the supply of wool from the farmers in the Pennines. Bradford and the other West Riding towns could supply cheaper labour than the traditional wool centres like Norwich, and packhorse trains incessantly crossed the hills and dales to the West Riding. Eventually the Yorkshire demand for wool became so great that it had to be brought from Scotland and Ireland too.

The wool was sorted and scoured, often by the woolstapler's family, and then distributed to the woolcombers. A quarter sessions complaint by Joseph Buck against two woolcombers alleged that they had stolen a pair of worsted wool combs and twenty-four pounds of wool, 'called worsted tops', from his workshop.

'Tops' of combed wool were then distributed to the handspinners. In fine weather, women and children could be seen everywhere wool-spinning outside the cottage doors. They used a simple one-thread wheel. The spun yarn was collected

7

The cloth-makers – Yorkshire weavers travelling to market with their woven pieces of cloth on the backs of their galloways.

The Leeds Cloth Hall, showing buyers and sellers of pieces of cloth made in the West Riding.

and passed on to the hand-loom weavers, who specialised in the weaving in their homes of many different types of cloth, including 'camlets, tammies, russels, serges and calimancoes'.

The woolstaplers' warehouses and piece rooms in their own houses would be filled with the finished pieces of cloth for display on market days. As well as their house, a barn and other outbuildings, the Bucks had a dyehouse, two warehouses and a shop at their premises at Host End. They also owned fields below the house, called Whitelands, Little Whitelands, Penny Oak, Crosse Close and the Ing.

In 1759, on John Buck's marriage, his father, by this time describing himself as a 'stuffmaker' or woollen cloth maker, gave him a handsome wedding present:

I do give to my son John Buck of the same place for the advancement of his future and for his convenience in carrying on or conducting business in partnership with me the debts which I have outstanding viz £800 and £600 = £1400.

It was normal practice to hand on private debts of this kind which could be used as security. Many prosperous businessmen were bankers in a small way, as a sideline to their main occupation.

Most of Jenny Buck's surviving letters are addressed to her niece Lidia Flower, and she gives a pleasing if sometimes tart description of the life of a wealthy young matron in the 1760s.

Writing briskly about her nephews, she praises 'your cousin Sam' as 'one of the Best Boys I ever saw – your Cousin Dawson [Humble] I doubt woud have been Equaly So had he been Less Indulgd . . .'

In summer her life contained a prodigious amount of visiting. She often wrote to Lidia about her peregrinations, on which her small daughter Sarah ['Sall'], born in 1760, accompanied her:

9

Sall and Myself have been for ten Days at Northowram and Only returned This Week . . . Sall and I have been a Week with Mama at Wither and left her pretty Well she thinks herself much better for her Scarboro journey . . . we got safe to Bradford after our Agreeable Visit and now return my Best Thanks to each Freind for the Kind Reception we had and can only say I shall be glad to return in the Best Manner I can at Bradford –

Lidia also enjoyed summer jaunts to see her Yorkshire relatives and their excursions included the fashionable watering place of Harrogate.

The roads were too bad for travelling during the winter, which made country life a tedious, lengthy imprisonment. To avoid it, people of means usually repaired to their 'Winter Habitation' in town – as did Mrs Dawson, Jenny's mother.

Although Jenny seldom mentions housekeeping details, she refers to the family servants from time to time:

I wrote to you from Leeds – but in case it should not be deliverd I thought it best to send John over to

Harrogate Wells, 1772.

10

Bradford . . . let Susie stay at her father's till I come home . . . Mr Buck presents his compliments and will take the Thirty Pounds you mentioned & as it is probable Franky will be at Gainsboro next week will order him to call for it . . .

A young woman in Jenny's position, married to a successful businessman, was not expected to occupy herself with the main work of housekeeping, although she directed the household and managed the stillroom, where she made cordials and wines – and sent them as presents:

I have just been Taping [tapping] a Cask of Genuine Birch Water and will send your uncle a little as soon as it is fit to put in the Bottle . . . I know this is what he used to like if he dare drink it . . .

Birch water, a popular drink of the period, was made by tapping the tree in order to collect the resinous fluid. When honey was added and the drink fermented, it resembled a home-made wine.

Jenny writes with obvious pleasure about her little daughter Sally, her toys and playmates, about clothes and china dishes, enjoyable food and drink:

Your Cousin bid me Insert her Love and is Much Obligd for Your Remembrance and Receivd Pero [Pierrot] with Pleasure she calls him Brother to Jack Tar . . .

In another letter she describes two little girls squabbling over their toys:

Sall bid me Insert her Love to all particularly her Cousin Lidia she and Miss Crossley are just now admiring the King and Queen which are I assure you Thought Amazing fine Things – that point about the Doll was settled to both their Satisfactions as Miss Crossley gave preference to the Go-Cart.

11

Clothes were another vital area of attention, and naturally members of the family lost no opportunity in buying their 'stuff', or wool fabric, at wholesale prices from John Buck:

My Dear Miss Flower shoud have had a More Early Answer to her past Epistle had I not waited till I coud meet with an Opportunity to send the Scarlet Stuff Mr Flower Desird might be sent to Gainsboro, which we have done by the Bearer of this — We coud not let you have just the Quantity mentiond as we always cut a Piece into Four Gowns and it woud have left a Remnant of no use and we thought a little More woud rather be a Convenience to you than Otherwise —

Sall bid me Insert her love and a Kiss to her cousin Lidia etc and will come to Gainsborough again to eat toasted Figs and All Good Things — Will my Good Girl send me the pattern of her Ruffles and Sprigs the same as Sister Todd's Apron — if you can send them to Mrs. Johnson's at Wakefield I will Order a person to call for them and think myself Obligd for your trouble . . .

The children were also dressed fashionably:

Sall bid me give her Love to her Cousin Lidia — She and Miss Charlotte is Much Obligd for your Letter and castors both which afforded Great Joy — she is now pretty well but has just had the Chickenpox and is to take Physick tomorrow — for a week she was really ill she says they are pretty Spots and will save one of them for her Cousin Lidia.

The castors which 'afforded Great Joy' were beaver hats, and perhaps muffs too. It was unusual for children as young as this to have fur hats, but this wealthy and much indulged little Yorkshire girl, and probably her friend 'Miss Charlotte' too, were luxuriously clad against the weather, like Russian children. Children's beaver hats were round and low-crowned, and often contained a mixture of coney and beaver for lightness.

Family difficulties for Jenny included the ever-present problem of what to do with assorted left-over aunts and cousins, who had to be bestowed in comfort somewhere, and usually at the family's expense. Widows and spinsters were usually dependent on the goodwill of their relatives. The unlucky ones could end up like a neighbour, 'poor Mrs Gleddle', who 'Dyed about 3 Weeks ago . . . I Believe she must have been thrown upon the town had not one or two of her Neighbours undertook to see her Decently Buryed – Sold Up what she had and is now paying the Debts . . .'

Jenny conscientiously attended to the family's problems, although with the occasional note of acerbity:

I have This Day been Removing Poor Cousin Matty Lupton from her Lodgings to Cousin Jessy's As Upon a Strict Enquiry I found the People she was with did not treat her with Common Humanity and coud not bear to have her Continued where I Believed she was not Well Used – my Aunt Hesketh hinted to me that she woud like to be with Mama – but I told her I Believd the Scheme woud not be Approved as at the Time my Mother Wanted the Most Assistance My Aunt had never found it in her Power to give it . . .

The persistent Aunt Hesketh got her own way, but then tried to 'settle' Cousin Sally too:

. . .with regard to my Aunt Hesketh it seems to be my Mother's Inclination to have her with her though without Doubt My Aunt being advanced in Life appears a Principal Objection – My Mother got to her Winter Habitation on Wednesday last and is pure well Aunt Hesketh is now with her but greatly perplexd about Cousin Sally . . . she gave a hint it woud be a great Satisfaction to her to have Sally in Mr Flower's family She begd I woud ask Sister Flower's advice what she thought best for her.

The family was anxious about Martha Flower, who had an

ominous 'Complaint in her Breast'. Although Lidia reported that Mrs Flower's friend Mrs Emlyn had looked at the problem and thought it 'owing to the Weather', the family knew better. We can understand the concern about Mrs Flower's illness, the course of which in those days would be impossible to arrest. Jenny felt that rural Gainsborough was not only far from good medical advice, but depressingly isolated. She wrote solicitously and often:

> . . . pray give my love to your mama and hope she does not neglect her Rideing out . . . tell me My Dear Miss Flower in your next if Your Mama's breast be really worse or My Sister's fears only lead her to think so . . . My Love to her and tell her your Grandmama and every Freind Honestly wishes she wd go to London as Gainsboro this Winter must be a little Dull when you are want of your good neighbours . . . In London I think I durst almost insure her better Health and Spirits . . . was sorry to hear Yr Mama had further Complaint

Where serious illness left the family powerless, at least the doctor's prescription for little Sally was a sensible enough antiseptic:

> All well but Myself a bad Cold Sall's Mouth now well she is still drinking Sea Water by Dr's directions

Jenny's worries about her ailing sister led her to make enquiries about a reliable maidservant. She sent a detailed report on the girl, but with her usual crispness, she wished the Flowers seemed more grateful:

> Dr Miss Flower, In my last I desird to know if Your mama was suited with Servants but in your Papa's last Letter no notice was took of it — I have just now been to enquire the Character of a Girl who has livd with Mrs Tarbaton who I Really think woud suit My Sister Extreamly Well in the place of Housemaid her Mistress says a Vast Deal in her Favour as to her Honesty

14

Temperance and Early Rising and that she has never been Wanting nor Rambled Out Half an Hour since she went to them.

Mistress, Master and two Young Children with an Apprentice is their Family at present they also keep a Cow and she has done their work Extreamly well . . . As to Wages if no Cloaths be given am pretty sure she will not come for 4 pound . . . Believe she is but About two and twenty but looks Strong and healthy.

By the time young Sally was four, John Buck felt secure enough about his future prosperity to plan a large and imposing mansion, which he began to build in 1764. He dreamed of a fit setting for the youngest daughter of wealthy Samuel Dawson and their lively little girl.

The family's happiness was evident in May the following year, when they all visited London together. John was on business, while Jenny and her daughter enjoyed sightseeing. Jenny wrote to her father in Leeds:

London May 30th 1765

Dear Sir,

Can with Pleasure inform You that we are all Well and Your Grand-daughter As well As You Yourself can wish and much Delighted with London and bid me tell You London is Beautifull Town she has a vast deal to tell You – Mr Buck also bid me insert his love but can Yet have no guess when he can leave this place, as he has not yet got Anything like an Order . . . we was so lucky as to meet the King in Our Way to London which was Vast Joy to Sall and bid me tell you she saw him alive – We are going this afternoon to See Greenwich Hospital so that you must excuse further Enlargement –

That summer was probably the high point of the family's life together, and when Sarah mused over these letters in her old age, she probably still recalled the pleasure of seeing King George III pass by in his carriage, and the sights of the

'Beautifull Town'. For a five year old country girl, London's streets must have bustled with life and excitement.

In December of the same year, 1765, Jenny had fallen ill. Feeling 'Weak and Rather Low', she answered Lidia's enquiries about her indisposition with a touch of pathos: 'You will excuse Blunders, Indeed I am Tired . . .' She went on:

> I am now pretty well Recovered tho Mr Winn still keeps me a Prisoner at Leeds but has given me leave to return home next Tuesday. I beleive from the Symptoms at first he Apprehended a bad Fever and an Ulcerated Sore Throat but have reason to be very Thankful these Complaints soon Abated – I Almost entirely Kept my bed for Severall Days which has made me Weak and Rather Low but doubt not if I keep free from Cold but a few Days will set me to Rights again.

Was Mr Winn, the medical man, the same impossibly beautiful spark of seven years before? It seems highly likely. Jenny went on:

> Mr. Buck came here last Night and tells me Mama had a Letter from London and that My Sister is at Present Mr Sharp's Patient. Sincerely wish the means he makes use of may have the desired Effect . . . pray write me Soon and be particular. Can you remember when I bought the China Dishes and Sauce Boats of the Man at Leeds if I paid him . . .

Debility may have been the cause of her forgetfulness over the bill for the china.

In February, 1766, Jenny's indulgent fondness for little Sall, now nearly six years old, made her write the following amusing letter to Lidia Flower, at the child's insistence. Her mother explained:

> On the Other side you will see a Letter from My Daughter every word her Own I Assure you & as you

16

may Guess without Any Assistance – the Writing in Part her Own . . .

Sall's letter is dated 'Feby 24th 1766':

> My Dr Cousin,
> I recd your Letter which I ought to have Answered long before. I am much Obliged to my Aunt for my Slip and it is very like Silver and I like the Pink Edges vastly – I think Mr Tommy Rawson will make you a very good Husband and then you will be our neighbour and Miss Crossley and me will Stay a Week with you and often step in – now this is to be All Joke – Master Roger has turned me quite off and I have got Master Dickey on – I suppose Our Lawyer will come a-Courting in Gracious Street and then you will be a Lawyeris – I can keep a secret if you will tell me one for as long as I live. I am
> Your Affectionate Cousin
> Sally Buck.

One can almost hear the little girl chattering eagerly to her Mama in an effort to get the beloved Lidia wedded. What happened to Lidia's marriage prospects we do not know, but Tommy Rawson, probably a member of the family which held the lordship of the manor of Bradford, would undoubtedly have been a good catch.

The happy days were now over for Jenny, John and little Sall. There is another document inside Jenny's transcription of her daughter's letter. An unknown hand, perhaps Lidia's, gives a detailed list of 'the letters of Jenny Dawson (Buck)'. The last, it explained, 'was probably written about a month or six weeks before her death. N.B. Miss Buck's letter is written in her mother's handwriting.'

Jenny Buck died in 1766 after seven years of marriage, leaving her husband John, a six year old daughter and a half-built mansion bereft of her presence.

17

my Dr Papa's ever Dutifull daughter

Sarah and John, 1770-1773

Townhill, the mansion house at the southern end of the family's Goodmansend estate, took four years to build. After the death of his young wife in 1766, John Buck must have roamed round his half-built house in despair over the collapse of his hopes to establish his family there. The building continued, however, and, according to his accounts, the house which eventually dominated the hill on the Wakefield road cost '£2,058-10s-8d'. It was built in classical style to a design by James Paine. Its south entrance looked on to a courtyard with a circular drive, a grassed area with a sundial, a large block of outbuildings, a shrubbery and garden. There was an octagonal room in the centre of the north side, and the terrace looked down across the fields towards the parish church. (Every vestige of this splendid mansion unfortunately vanished during the expansion of Bradford into a large industrial city.) Townhill was typical of the substantial houses built for the 'masters' of the eighteenth century, many of which still survive in West Yorkshire. The men who built them were well-travelled and well-educated. Their knowledge of markets in Europe and the colonies ensured that though they were provincial they were not parochial, and this enabled them to lay the foundations of the next century's thriving export trade.

As their prosperity grew they built fine houses, but these never lost their close connection with business. There were outbuildings beside them where trade could be carried on,

Artist's impression, from the drawings of architect James Paine, of Townhill from the north. The house stood on the Wakefield road, looking down the hill towards Bradford.

and could include dyehouses, warehouses, drying rooms, shops and counting houses. The semi-industrial complex also contained the master's farm, with grazing land for his horses and cows, pigs and sheep, to provide food for his family's needs.

John Buck's house was not inhabited till 1770, according to a memorandum of his son-in-law William Whittaker. John, his daughter Sarah, her nurse and their servants were the occupants, but the establishment must have sadly lacked the presence of a gracious mistress. Within two years, John had

Artist's impression, from the drawings of architect
James Paine, of the main south entrance of Townhill.

decided that it was time Sarah went to a young ladies'
academy to further her education. She was eleven years old.

Sarah was sent as a boarder to Crofton Old Hall School
near Wakefield. The school, a private establishment for
young ladies, was run by the Reverend David Traviss and his

wife Margaret. The Travisses had two daughters: Ann, who was married to Thomas Faber, the Vicar of Calverley near Bradford; and Caroline, who was a few years older than Sarah. The Travisses were to become great friends for young Miss Buck, and the family seems to have taken the place to some extent of the mother she had lost.

Crofton Old Hall was a handsome house with extensive grounds and a lake, in a pretty country village. Although in Sarah's time it was a family home for the Travisses as well as an informal boarding school, it remained a private school for many generations, but was finally demolished during the 1970s. Modern houses have now obliterated the green fields round the house, but the lake and vestiges of the gateway can still be seen.

The school the Travisses started at Crofton was to have a distinguished future in the early nineteenth century. A pupil

Artist's impression of Crofton Hall School, near
Wakefield.

21

who arrived there a few years after Sarah, Richmal Mangnall, remained as a governess and eventually became the head-mistress.

Miss Mangnall became a celebrity in 1798 when she published, at first anonymously, her textbook *Historical and Miscellaneous Questions*, a general knowledge questions book which became a best-seller in young ladies' academies and was eventually published by Longmans.

Miss Mangnall's prospectus of 1818 survives, so it is possible to glean some idea of what boarding school girls at Crofton might be expected to learn, though perhaps the syllabus was less formal in the Travisses' day. Her pupils of 1818 were 'boarded and instructed in plain and fancy work for thirty-three guineas per annum', and 'entrance to the house and teachers' was £3 13s 6d. The pupils were described as 'ladies', and the juniors as 'little ladies'.

Each 'lady' had to bring with her a list of necessary equipment and the terms of the masters were stated. They were responsible for 'English grammatically, writing and Accompts, Geography, French, Music and Italian, at fees ranging from ten shillings and sixpence per quarter to five guineas a year'.

Under the Travisses, Sarah's lessons could well have followed a similar pattern. Her letters contain requests for her bills to be paid by her father. These probably pertain to the boarding fees and to the extra lessons for dancing, art and music given by visiting masters.

Whatever else she learned at school, her lessons in English were successful, for she writes confidently and in a flowing script, her thoughts fresh and well-expressed. At eleven Sarah wrote in a reasonably graceful hand, although her characters are childishly large. By the following year, 1773, her handwriting had matured into an elegant copper-plate, and her letters are beautifully laid out.

Girls seldom received a classical education, but in a way they benefited by studying a rudimentary version of a modern syllabus, including modern languages, geography, history

22

and music. Sometimes they may even have gained the advantage over their brothers, whose endless studies of the classics left less time for other subjects.

Wakefield was the place to go for 'finishing' a young lady from one of the smaller West Riding towns. It was a sophisticated and important centre in the eighteenth century and figures in all the topographical works of the time as a handsome, clean and 'opulent' county town, with splendid brick mansions built by wool merchants and woolstaplers. It had three broad streets, Westgate, Northgate and Kirkgate. The wealthy had their town houses in Westgate, and in Northgate lived those of genteel breeding who had to manage on smaller incomes, such as widows, younger brothers and retired military men. Some of the Georgian town houses for which Westgate was distinguished still stand, as do many of the eighteenth century warehouses in nearby streets.

The letters Sarah wrote to her father from school are full of spirit, although they always express a correctly dutiful attitude. 'I am my Dr Papa's ever Dutifull daughter' she

Westgate, Wakefield, in the eighteenth century.

would finish her letters, and 'Pray give my duty to my Grandpapa and Grandmamma – Pray give my duty to my Uncle and Aunt Todd'.

They pleased her father so much that he kept them by him, and even wrote some of his own calculations and notes on them. They give an illuminating glimpse into the life of a schoolgirl of the upper middle classes, surrounded by wealth and influence. But she was still an orphan, and there is sometimes a wistful tone to her letters, with hints of homesickness. Her holidays were often spent at school, while her father, fighting loneliness but apparently not feeling the need of his daughter's company, diverted himself in Scarborough or London.

In the Christmas holidays at the end of her first term, however, she began a letter, bubbling with excitement, to Caroline Traviss, who was staying with their schoolfriend Miss Stovin. The letter was directed to 'Mrs. James Stovin's, At the Hall Croft, Doncaster', and written on a very large sheet of paper.

With characteristic *élan* Sarah described the school's holiday dramatic entertainment, perhaps organised for girls like herself who did not go home – and added a witty schoolgirl insult to their friend 'Stovin':

> Well, dear Caroline, you can't imagine with what pleasure I write to you. My governess is very good to us and we are all very merry – Well now I must tell you our characters – Lady Bingley Miss Sarah, Lord Bingley Miss Close, Lady Fanny Bingley Fanny Hague, The Old Maid Miss Hardman, Lord Burlington Miss Swan, Lady Burlington your old Friend myself;
>
> Pray tell Stovin I am much obligd for the Toffy she sent and for her Complyments & I daresay (Tho I don't intend it as a Complyment) that Miss Stovin if there is a Masquerade will be much admired by everyone . . .

Mrs Traviss was indulgent enough to allow Sarah to help the cook while lessons were over for the holidays, and Sarah's

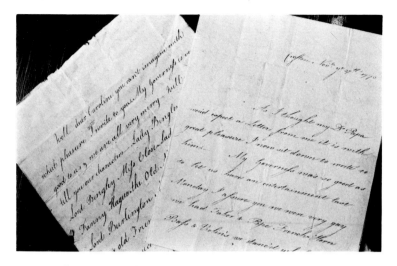

Letters from Sarah Buck to her father John Buck,
from Crofton School, 1772-3.

letter gives an amusing glimpse of the bustle of the Travisses'
kitchen:

> Well now I must thank my dearest Caroline for her
> good Cake – I have just been stoning some Raisins for
> our dinner for you must know we live like Princes – we
> had a grand wedding here of Furbisher's daughter, and
> they were so fond of Raspberry Jam that tho my
> governess gave them half a pot they were not content.

Sarah's Christmas holidays of 1772 were not without
further treats, as she relates next:

> On Tuesday I received a letter from my Papa in which
> he informs me that Mrs Liversedge was so good as to
> ask my Papa to let me go to spend a few Days there
> these holidays – my governess was so good as to get us
> all tickets for the concert and we shall all go on
> Wednesday –

Part of Sarah's education, on John Buck's instructions, was

to consist of staying with Wakefield ladies and accompanying them on their calls and entertainments. They were kind to the little motherless girl who needed lessons in decorum and etiquette.

When Sarah broke off her holiday letter to Caroline Traviss in favour of more interesting pursuits, Mrs Traviss, who kept a motherly and indulgent eye on her charge, used up the rest of the large sheet of paper, and described taking Sarah visiting with her:

Meeting with this epistle at my return home on Sunday I thought I might as well write on as the above scribe is at Wakefield and Mrs Susey with whom she is I fancy a good deal engaged. I left her there by Mr. Buck's desire and shall send for her on Saturday as her Wardrobe will do very well – but at Wakefield one dirtys ten times more than at home . . .

Mrs Burton insisted Miss Buck should stay there while I did, and was more than commonly civil to her, indeed the little girl behaved very well.

The Burtons owned the Wakefield raw wool market in Westgate, and Mrs Burton would be a wealthy widow when Sarah knew her. The Wakefield ladies seem to have demanded formality and frequent changes into appropriate dress. Sarah had to learn these customs as well as good manners. Naturally she would be expected to sit quietly while her elders conversed and answer clearly when she was spoken to.

Sarah was also invited to visit the ladies of Wakefield during the 'Season' in the middle of September, leaving the quiet country village of Crofton for a lively social centre. Each year there were three days of races, and the race course at Outwood (now long vanished) had a 'grandstand for the gentlemen and booths for the company'. On the first and third nights of race week, assemblies were held at the White Hart assembly rooms, and included card parties, dances and

dinners. Wakefield's Strafford Gardens were a miniature version of London's popular Vauxhail Gardens.
The theatre also played throughout September. Tate Wilkinson, Wakefield's celebrated actor-manager, arrived there in 1774 with his company from Beverley, and decided to stay, thinking it an excellent place to risk his future. He described the Wakefield *beau monde* in glowing terms:

> The neighbourhood of Wakefield is genteel, opulent and numerous, and whenever they choose to be unanimous and attend the theatre, a stranger, even from London, would be astonished at beholding the number of gentlemen's elegant carriages attending the Theatre to convey their wealthy and spirited owners to their neighbouring villas, several of which may be termed palaces.

'When I was at Mrs. Lumb's', Sarah wrote to her father on 'October ye 9th 1773', 'she treated me to see the model of Paris it is very well worth seeing – we have had a curious machine here called the Chronoscope in imitation of Coxes Museum it is exceedingly pretty –'

The 'Chronoscope' which caught Sarah's fancy was a marvel of ingenuity first displayed in 1772 at Coxes Museum in London. James Cox was a jeweller who devised extremely elaborate clocks and watches in fantastic style, often incorporating automata. The Chronoscope was one of his most elaborate contraptions. About eight feet high, it consisted of a mound of figures of animals, men and women, fruit and flowers, finished in precious metals, enamels, lapidary work and jewellery. An elephant with a mobile trunk moved round a circular track bearing a striking, chiming and repeating clock, dragons flapped their wings and dropped pearls, music played, and the whole thing was on wheels.

The Lumbs were one of the most important of the Wakefield wool families. There were so many branches of the family that it is impossible to say which Mrs Lumb

27

entertained Sarah, but the circles in which they all moved were certainly the best in this prosperous town.

The senior branch of the Lumb family had a large mansion at Silcoates, built in 1748 by John Lumb. In 1773 it was inhabited by two lonely gentlemen, Mr Lumb and his son Thomas. Sarah's Mrs Lumb may have taken the little girl to Silcoates in her carriage at least once during her holiday, perhaps to pay a morning call. It had a handsome red and cream brick façade, framed by lawns and trees. The graceful drawing room still remains as it was in the 1770s. Sarah would sit here demurely, her ears alert for the polite chat of her elders. (Silcoates House has lasted into the late twentieth century in a state of elegant preservation, and is now the headmaster's house at Silcoates School.)

Artist's impression of the town house of the Lumb
family on Westgate, Wakefield. The house is
still standing.

28

Sarah could also have stayed at the large Lumb family town house in Westgate – also still surviving, and distinguished by its handsome pedimented façade. How Mrs Lumb entertained her twelve year old guest is not certain – perhaps the amusements were mostly of the educational kind, like the 'model of Paris'. In 1773, when Sarah's schoolgirl visits are chronicled, plays were enacted in what Tate Wilkinson, the actor-manager, disparagingly described as 'a shabby theatre in Bull Yard'. The new theatre was built soon after Tate Wilkinson arrived, so it is possible that Sarah would attend performances there before she left school.

She undoubtedly joined in the social events during the celebrations of race week and Christmas. A later letter of 1775, written by Sarah's father John Buck, also mentions that Sarah has gone to Mrs Lumb's for 'Race Week', and at fifteen, still enjoying her visits to Wakefield society, she would certainly be considered a grown-up young lady.

Although Wakefield itself was considered a handsome, well-built town, its surroundings were still very rural, and the roads, in spite of the new turnpikes, were voted by most travellers to Yorkshire to be 'execrable'. Horace Walpole, a reluctant visitor, said of the Yorkshire roads that 'they mend them or should I say spoil them with large stones and branches . . .'

Travelling from Crofton to Wakefield, a distance of only three miles, was difficult in winter. Mrs Traviss disliked it heartily, as she explained to Caroline:

> I commend your prudence in having no Nocturnal Rambles – those I had were not of my own seeking the Streets are so bad and Mrs. Burton's horse kicks so I was often obliged to walk home by which means I caught a severe cold, and she also tho she continues to go out grumbling every day. I shall not venture to Banktop this Vacancy for ridding on Horseback is too much for me, such long journeys in Winter being not always fitting . . .

Mrs Traviss's curious usage of 'Vacancy' for holidays may have been based on the fact that she came from a Huguenot family and affected a French style of writing. She also viewed the whole uncomfortable business of riding with dislike and even terror, like many another English lady of the day. Ann Faber, the vicar's wife, was a different and bolder type, however. Mrs Traviss shuddered at her hunting exploits, and wrote disgustedly to Caroline:

> This Weather will I think put a stop to your Sister's feats of Horsemanship Riding is a chearful and Healthy exercise but as to chassing the Fox I cannot say it comes within the female character . . .

The problem for the faint-hearted was that a carriage was not always available. Going to town therefore, even for a few ribbons, could involve getting dressed for riding and then handling the huge and awkward brute successfully. Often it was preferable to stay at home, especially in winter.

In summer getting around was not much easier, even though the turnpikes were supposed to have improved matters. In July 1773 Sarah wrote that 'we had a very pleasant ride from Wakefield to Crofton, but the New Road [the turnpike] was very dirty from Bradford to Wakefield.'

Lessons are never mentioned in Sarah's letters from school – she concentrates on the more interesting side of life. On the 'July ye 6th 1773', she wrote:

> Dear Papa, As Miss Traviss told me you desired I would write, I take this opportunity of doing as you wished me. Pray must I have my suit of Linnen made up that I have been working to my Silk Coat [petticoat]. If I am pray let me know –

A little girl's 'suit' consisted of a sleeved bodice and a separate outer petticoat, or a sleeved bodice with an open skirt worn over a petticoat. The 'Linnen' was for summer wear, and was one of the lighter and less restricting styles of dress being brought in for children during the latter part of the century. By 'working', Sarah means her needlework, a major part of her education.

On the 27th July she wrote again, hopeful that her father was coming to call for her, but no doubt admonished by her governesses not to whine:

Dear Papa, I receivd my Dr papa's 2 Letters at the same time & am much obliged to you for them – I had got my Linnen in readiness before I receivd yours, as I was in daily expectation of a summons. I shall be very happy to see you with or without wig but as I imagine you must have had particular reasons best known to yourself, or you would not have resisted the intreaties of your freinds – Mrs Faber called here – she was so good as to bring the parcel you sent, for which I am obliged to you – Mrs Faber has two sets of curls, one powdered, one unpowdered, but no toupee – Miss Traviss has bought me a Bonnet and Tippet as you desired – Pray favour me with a few lines soon in the meantime I am my Dr papa's dutiful and affectionate daughter, Sarah Buck.

Caroline's sister Ann Faber, although a vicar's wife, seems to have been a lively and fashionable young woman as well as a keen horsewoman. Sarah was undoubtedly fascinated, as most children of her age must have been, by the extravagant hair fashions for both ladies and gentlemen. Elaborately powdered wigs were the height of modishness in 1773, and her father's new wig was a source of intense interest to the little girl, not to mention Mrs Faber's two sets of curls. The 'toupee' was a special hair-piece set at the front of the head, which enabled the elaborately dressed hair to be lifted to an exaggerated height.

John Buck ordered his daughter's clothes to be chosen and bought by the Travisses, and sent regular presents of food for Sarah, her governesses and friends. Sarah's letters are full of her thanks for these gifts:

31

I got a basket which I am certain came from so good a freind as yourself. Miss Traviss, Miss Walker and I supped on one of the birds and did not forget to drink your health.

Like most gentlemen of the day, John Buck enjoyed hunting and shooting, and his presents frequently consisted of part of his bag. In November, Sarah thanked him for 'the woodcock which was very good' and early in December for 'the partridge and Cake – my governess desires I should thank you for the Oysters and we drank your health'. Rather pathetically, Sarah continually hoped that her father would come to visit her, though he apparently made excuses:

I beg you will not put yourself to the least inconveniencey in regard to coming to see me, but when it suits you, you may suppose I should have no objection –

She sounded even more rueful when John Buck, the widower, took himself to Scarborough in September 1773. The idea of a seaside holiday nowadays without the children seems very strange, but Scarborough was then a fashionable watering place for adults. She addressed 'Mr Buck, at Mrs Turner's, Scarborough':

Dear Papa, I began to think the time long before I had the pleasure of hearing from my Dearest Papa – I was impatient to know how you did – I hope you will spend your time agreeably at Scarbro the players will add to the amusement of the place & when you can spare the time I hope often to hear from you –

Sarah knew very well why her father frequented the fashionable spas, and in her own way, tried to help. In one letter she hints that 'I hear Miss Browning and Miss Lister are going to Harrowgate I suppose you would not dislike being one of the company'.

In another she adds a saucy postscript: 'P.S. Miss Walker sends her respects and if you are not engaged, has thoughts of spending the holidays with you.' She also kept an interested eye on John's social life, remarking that 'A person was here this morning who told me you had an entertainment on Saturday last – I hope you was very chearful'. A letter from her father must have contained a description of this party, for soon afterwards she wrote: 'I was glad you was so much entertained by your company' and added, in a phrase which sums up the anxieties of her governesses, who were very much aware of the young and wealthy Bradford widower, 'my governess says she finds you are not for admitting Old Women, so you did not wish her to be amongst the number'.

Late in November, the girls also had an 'entertainment', and Sarah wrote excitedly, her Bradford idiom surfacing in the use of 'while':

> My Dear Papa, My governess was so good as to let us have an entertainment last Monday. I assure you we were very gay we had Tabor and Pipe, French Horn, Bass and Violins we danced while nine o'clock and were exceedingly merry – We break up the 18th of next month and my governess has provided me a companion a little girl – Miss Traviss has sent the Clasp which she will be obliged to you to get fixed to the Tablet of Memory.

With Christmas again approaching, Sarah felt homesick and not unnaturally wanted to see her father. A brave face had to be put on things, but mentioning the 'Tablet of Memory' for her mother's grave gave her father a pointed hint about his daughter's feelings:

> I should have been very glad to have come home these holidays, but as there is a necessity of your being away you know I shall be very happy to stay here.
> Mrs Faber and Master Stanley will be here and I shall have nice Nurseing pray be so good as to send me two packs of cards – you said you woud get me something to make baskets on pray be so good as to remember –

P.S. Pray be so good as to send me some Scarlet Stuff for a petticoat – I will let you know by Mrs Jobson about the Harpsichord.

A week before Christmas, Sarah was ready to let the idea of the harpsichord go:

. . . in regard to the Harpsichord Mr Jobson says it is made of unseasoned wood the keys are very bad it will not stand in tune. . .be so good as to send me a parcel of magazines to amuse me this Xmas – I have quite worn out my Sheets, be so kind as to send me a good, strong pair –

It seems rather heartless to us that the little girl should have been left forlornly at school during the Christmas holidays while her father went up to London. But in 1773, Christmas was a less sentimental festivity than today, and it was probably not with much sense of deprivation that Sarah settled philosophically for 'two packs of cards' and 'a parcel of magazines' to amuse her during the vacation.

The Travisses and the cheerful Mrs Faber and her son could be relied on to provide plenty of family fun, or 'nice nurseing', as Sarah so quaintly puts it.

*to the Great Surprize, amaze or astonishment
of the Bradfordians*

Caroline and Sarah, 1775-1780

With his daughter away at school, John Buck tried to divert himself with visits to 'Harrowgate', London and 'Scarboro'. He gave 'entertainments' and invited company, his social efforts recorded for us in Sarah's letters. But his loneliness and depression continued, as he shows touchingly in the letter he wrote in September 1775 to Lidia Flower, the niece who had been his lost wife Jenny's confidante. After a bleak homecoming from a visit to London, John wrote wearily to Lidia from Townhill:

> As I promised you to write I sit down without having any Thing interesting to communicate, farther than that I got home well last night, found my father and mother well, and a Letter from Sally Buck [his daughter Sarah], wherein she informs me that Mrs Lumb has given her an Invitation to spend the next (being Race Week) with her, and that her Governess has consented to let her go for 2 or 3 days

He was forbidden wine, probably because of gout, and business seemed less than exhilarating as he spent long solitary hours on his accounts:

> I am now entered upon the dull old scene of Books and Columns, have wrote Today till I scarce can hold the Pen, and would leave the Counting House, but know not what to do with myself — for Neighbours have I none,

that I can sit an Hour with, and go into Company I
cannot because I cannot drink –

Mr Bischoff, a well-known Leeds merchant and a friend of
the family, also wrote to Lidia Flower during this time, telling
her that 'Mr. Buck took a ride over to us last week, the
meeting was affecting and brought all the idea of our lost
friend to us anew.'
John seems to have been a conscientious parent, full of
good advice for his daughter. Sarah's character as she grew
up was lively and enthusiastic. She had extravagant hopes of
accomplishment, but sometimes lacked staying power, as her
father pointed out. When she asked for yet more lessons, he
admonished:

> I did not think you unreasonable in your request,
> there is no-one wishes or desires to see you more
> accomplished than myself – I only thought you would
> have more Irons in the Fire than you could attend to,
> and to call in more Masters than you have leisure to
> reflect on their Instructions in their absence and try to
> do by yourself *till you can do it* what they have been
> teaching you, will answer no end, and you'll be the same
> when they leave you, as you was before they came . . .

He disapproved of her tendency to sluggardly behaviour,
and made clear his wishes on early rising:

> How will these hours suit you when you return to
> Townhill? We must have you to breakfast at 7 instead
> of 10, and I wish now the mornings are light and warm
> you would accustom yourself to practise on the Harpsi-
> chord and make yourself perfect in everything your
> Master shews you before he comes again – for there is
> no need of being a Solomon to understand Music – I
> know you will reply, what must those be then that do
> not understand it after many years indefatigable pains
> have been taken with them? to which I also have the

Answer – and shall be glad to find you are not classed among them –

As they grew up, Sarah and Caroline Traviss remained friends. They enjoyed visiting Calverley vicarage, near Bradford, where Caroline's sister Ann and her husband, the Reverend Thomas Faber, kept a more cheerful establishment than lonely Townhill. Sarah and Caroline appear to have been an independent pair. Surprisingly, they were allowed to go out unchaperoned, much to the delight of a young gentleman who met them one moonlit evening, probably on their way back to Bradford from Crofton. Sarah and Caroline had found themselves, like many an unwary traveller, held up at the tollbooth for lack of their turnpike money.

It was not unusual for altercations, even riots, to take place as unsuspecting local people discovered that they must pay to use the new turnpikes. The gallant Mr Thode naturally seized the opportunity to make their acquaintance by offering his assistance. The letter he wrote afterwards was carefully preserved, probably in Caroline's 'private cabinet' and undoubtedly hidden from parental scrutiny. The letter is undated but was probably written about 1776:

> Mr Thode returns his compliments to your Ladyships B. . . and T. . ., and is much obliged for the pains they have taken in trying his patience as well as disappointing him of the contents – The same he can't look upon in any other Way but as a Repaying of the Turnpike money, or as a Recompence for the Care he had taken at a moonlight night – In both cases Mr Thode is truly sorry he can't accept the contents, and flatters himself the moonlight ladies won't condemn his behaviour when he takes the liberty of returning the inclosed – any other thing but money would have been gratefully receivd and kept as a High Treasure –

Mr Thode's literary style is cumbersome – perhaps he was

too rushed for elegant composition. The following morning he had changed his mind, and wrote at the bottom of the page: 'Monday morning. Turn Over.' Overleaf he continued:

> Just as Mr Thode is going to inclose the treasure he upon a second Consideration thinks it unpardonable to return a thing coming from *so sweet hands* as those of my lady T. . . and should it even be money, and tho it is the first Instance that such a thing was presented to him by the fair sex, yet if your ladyship will be kind enough to overlook and forgive his former Observations, Mr Thode intends laying it by in his private cabinet and keep it in memory of those heavenly creatures with whom he had the pleasure to spend one of the most happiest of Evenings, as long as a Blood Vessel is circulating in him. . . In great haste . . .

Who the courteous but physiologically confused Mr Thode was there is no inkling, but the girls must have giggled over his letter and kept it carefully as a souvenir of the moonlight adventure of their youth.

While they were enjoying life, John Buck remained solitary, but his thoughts turned frequently towards remarriage. He wrote to Lidia:

> I am tired out with this mode of life and think I will soon put a period to it – but as that cannot be done without the Consent of some fair Female, I am still obliged to exercise my Patience, and fly to my old Friend Hope, who has given me Subsistence for many Years –

The answer to his problem of loneliness was eventually to be found right under his nose. He fell in love with his daughter's best friend – a development which may at first have caused some eyebrows to be raised. On the 27th February 1777, he married Caroline Traviss at Crofton. She was probably in her late twenties, and he around fifty. The arrangement suited Sarah beautifully. She was delighted at finding herself with a young stepmother who would certainly not prove to be a severe guardian.

Sarah was visiting her London relatives when the news came of the first child's arrival. John's story was sad, but the occurrence was not unusual:

Townhill. Dec 23, 1777

My Dear Girl,

Mrs Todd would inform you that your Mother was delivered of a dead little Girl this morning betwixt 3 and 4 o'clock, after a very sore Labour ever since Sunday evening, and before she begun was so well as to read a Sermon – since she got her Bed has rested very well, and I hope is in the ready road of Recovery, was it not for the Loss of her little one, which Mrs Wright pronounced to be dead 2 Hours before it made its appearance, and she thinks it got strangled in turning for the Birth, for it had the appearance of a healthy, fleshy and thriving Child and was full grown and perfect, and as like what you were when you made your first appearance, as you can suppose two peas in a pod – Caroline receivd your Letter this morning, and has been so well as to read it to me, for I could not read it myself, and desires her kindest love and Remembrance to each . . .

Cool Caroline seems to have been, strangely, less affected than her emotional husband by the event. The house was full of relatives – Caroline's mother and sister, as well as Miss Fenton, the nurse, looked after her. There is no mention of a doctor.

Sarah seems to have stayed in London with her aunts and uncles, the Flowers and the Todds, for most of that year, probably to give her a taste of London society and introduce her to suitable beaux. A few months later, in the spring, another letter from John Buck to his daughter revealed that Caroline had recovered only too well from her disappointment and very lengthy convalescence:

Part of a letter from John Buck to his daughter
Sarah Buck, 1777.

I set out at one o'Clock on Tuesday morning and got
home on Wednesday evening, when I found your Mother
expecting me and very well and what is most wonderful
she had been that afternoon with Miss Fenton at the
Card Assembly – the latter left us on Friday after being
with us above 4 months. She was almost naturalized to

the place and the House at first was not like itself without her. What will you say when I tell you I am a Widower again? – but if not altogether, my situation calls to my remembrance those days, for your Mother and I are like two Buckets, no sooner do I come home than she flys away, and pleads her being a close Housekeeper in my absence for the Practice.

Caroline, it seemed, was too young and flighty for a serious businessman much older than herself. She was clearly bored with being a 'close Housekeeper', and John suspected that she cared less for him than before. In her husband's absence, she may already have been casting a flirtatious eye in the direction of John's younger partner.

Francis Duffield became John Buck's partner at least as early as 1774, as is evidenced by the day book of another Bradford businessman, the stone merchant Abraham Balme, who had supplied building materials for Townhill. In 1778 he has entries for 'lime for Mr Buck's wall 0-7-4 [7s 4d] and 1-14-0 [£1 14s] to the carters'. Balme also acted as a private bank in discounting bills of exchange, the normal method of commercial payment. He has several entries between 1774 and 1779 for bills payable in fifty or sixty days by 'Buck and Duffield', but discounted by Balme and paid immediately to creditors like Jonas Midgley and Thomas Feather, probably weavers, who needed their money quickly.

John complained again of Caroline's restless behaviour:

Your Mother took off on Wednesday before 6 o'Clock in the morning to go to Crofton for a Week and took up Mrs Faber at Mrs Gott's where she was waiting at that time in the morning –

Sarah's return to Townhill must have lifted the spirits of her father and young stepmother, however, and the mansion would at least have a livelier atmosphere. Sarah and Caroline were much occupied with their latest gowns, and with planning entertainments and visits.

In November 1779, when they were all getting ready for the assembly at Bradford, there was a crossing of swords between the fashion-conscious daughter and her staider father. Nineteen year old Sarah had grown into a witty and accomplished young woman, who undoubtedly succeeded in getting her own way after an hour spent at her writing desk. When she gave her father the beautifully-composed petition, in perfect legal terminology, how could he resist her?:

The Prayr and Petition of S.B. to Wear
a Gause [gauze] Apron

Whereas the petition of S. Buck Spinster of the parish of Bradford humbly sheweth Tuesday evening of this present Novr. being the Assembly at Bradford when the inhabitants of the aforesaid Town do meet to Dance, eat, drink, Card and Carouse according to their various taste, the whole family of the Bucks consisting of Caroline, John and the aforementioned Sarah Buck harboured certain intentions of going riding and walking to the said Assembly, to which purpose Sarah intended wearing a Satin of a pink, red or redish Color which was decorated with a trimming of Gause and Flowrs, but as the aforesaid Trimming grew rather ancient and more-over was a good deal soild by frequent use or wear, the said Sarah was preparing to unrip, unpick or take off the said Trimming and put in its place a Gause Apron which Apron being a good deal tore or disfigured coud not be worn at any place of Genteel Rendezvous or resort. She therefore thought it for prudential motives adviseable to put it on at the aforesaid Assembly or meeting, for it was not only a saving scheme but a reputable looking one, as the aforesaid pink, red or redish Satin woud shine with great Brilliance through the above mentioned Gause to the Great Surprize, amaze or astonishment of the Bradfordians, and as Sarah Buck was preparing to unrip, unpick or take off the said

42

The old market building, Bradford. Assemblies were
held in the upper floor rooms.

trimming, John Buck in the Nick of Time put a stop to
these (as she thought Innocent) proceedings to her utter
amaze, for woud any man gainsay that a Gause Apron
is not Genteeler and Handsomer and prettier than a
ragged and Dirty Gause Trimming, and moreover
consistent with oeconomical schemes – but will contrast
this case with another viz – supposing the said John
Buck was going on a Pheasant Shooting party and had
two old guns made for the destruction of the aforesaid
Fowls, and he prefering one to the other and wishing to
get it wore out, was busy in Cleaning and taking and
removing the Dirt, was suddenly prevented by one
Ignorant of the art of Shooting Flying. Woud he not seek
Justice – for the same reason does Sarah Buck send this
Petition to the End that it may be granted and yr.
Petitioner shall ever pray.

Silk gauze aprons were the height of fashion in 1779, and
the 'oeconomical', re-fashioned red satin gown was worn at
the assembly, no doubt to the plaudits of her friends, and 'to

the Great Surprize, amaze or astonishment' of at least a few of the Bradfordians. Her father kept her petition as carefully as he did her schoolgirl letters. She probably reminded him of his sprightly lost Jenny in her youth.

Her cousin Lidia Flower disappears from the family story about this time, but Aunt Todd, Sarah's mother's sister, wrote assiduously and at length. In February the following year, 1780, Sarah received a letter congratulating her on recovery from an illness. Aunt Todd was pious, sententious, but affectionate. If her anxiety seems excessive, it is as well to remember that, in 1780, even what seemed at first to be minor ailments could be fatal:

My Dear Girl – Your Father's first Letter informing us what were the Symptoms of Your Disorder was rather alarming and as our Spirits were depressed by the unfavourable Account – so were they proportionately Elated when by his kind repeated favours we received the much wished for Confirmation that your Complaint was not only Abated – but that all these anxious Apprehensions of danger were removed –

Aunt Todd felt that Sarah's survival merited some moral reflections:

Now my Dear Miss Buck no doubt these Dispensations are Lessons of Instruction Calculated to make us both wiser and better – and though I woud be sorry to be too serious a Monitor . . . a true sense of the Divine Goodness in your late preservation will convince you of the propriety of being ever Watchfull – how necessary and Usefull it will be to cultivate Habbitts of frequent and Serious Reflection – but you want not my Remonstrances – and if they are deemd Unreasonable – let Sincerity of Heart Dictated by the Motives of love and Affection plead the Appologie that its plainness requires and obtain your Pardon for its freedom –
    I was very happy well knowing you under the

44

Influence of an anxious and affectionate Father and the Watchfull Officious Care of Mrs Buck – who so kindly to you discharges the Parentall Office and by a freindship so mutual and so confirmed that youll long live happy in the firm and lasting possession of them

Comically solemn, the endearing Aunt Todd's rolling sentences also confirm that Caroline was expecting another child. This child was Sarah's half-brother, John William Buck:

I was very happy to hear Mrs Buck enjoys so good a share of health and Spirits – and that no unfavourable Contingency may cast a gloom on her present pleasing prospects

Aunt Todd's efforts to perform 'the Epistoliary' art caused her much stress and fatigue, and she often lost her grasp of syntax, spelling and sense. She even dreaded the arrival of letters from the family, which again put her under the necessity of replying. '. . . my Talent for Writing', she confessed, 'was ever slow and by Dislike becomes more Tardy'.

John Buck died soon afterwards, in 1780, according to a memorandum written by his grandson. It is not certain whether he ever saw the new baby, a healthy little boy. He did not leave a will, and anxious family consultations were undertaken in order to guard the interests of his heirs, Sarah and the baby John William. They are all recorded in the Wakefield Registry of Deeds, the oldest registry of property in the country, established in 1704, and one of only five similar offices. It was popular with the owners of small wool firms, who were glad to have a clearly registered title which enabled them to borrow money on their properties.

Two 'memorials' (summaries of the deeds) in the registry record the arrangements in 1781 for the large property inheritance of John William Buck, infant, at Denholme near Bradford. His trustees included his mother Caroline Buck and her brother-in-law Thomas Faber, the vicar of Calverley. Many years later, J W Buck was to mourn the death of the trusty Mr Faber, who had always looked after 'my estates in Denholme'.

Another memorial records the arrangements for the inheritance of Sarah Buck, which included 'closes and parcels of land' in Bradford. The invaluable Mr Faber became one of her trustees also. Sarah inherited Townhill, but Caroline continued to live there, being joined eventually by her second husband, Francis Duffield, John Buck's former partner, whom she married in 1782.

The picture of Sarah preparing her gown for the Bradford assembly is the last glimpse of her for several years. In 1786, she married William Whittaker, 'of Manchester, merchant, formerly of Bradford', and a memorial records the marriage settlement between Sarah, William Whittaker and her trustees. How and where Sarah and William met is not known. The heiress and the charming young businessman may have met at one of the lively Bradford assemblies. William's early life remains a mystery, but much anguished letter-writing was to illuminate his later years.

one of my 'enlivening Scrawls' by way of douceur

Manchester and Bradford, 1786-1794

Sarah and William set up their home in Manchester after their marriage. They had two children – William, born in March 1791, and Sarah, born in October 1792. Both children were christened at St Anns Church, near the family's winter home and business premises in Brown Street, a busy, crowded lane off Market Street. William's warehouse was in nearby Marsden Street, which had been the home of Manchester's first theatre. The Whittakers also rented a farm at Moss Side, as it was the general practice among the well-to-do Manchester merchants to live out of town during the summer.

Manchester as William and Sarah knew it in the seven years of their life there was a jumble of old and new buildings, black and white houses, and narrow, cobbled streets with a few squares and churchyards. St Anns Square, King Street and St James's Square were considered the best situations for important business warehouses and offices. Spring Gardens and Fountain Street still recall the eighteenth century town's water supply. Concert Lane was named from the Gentlemen's Concert, a hall built in 1777 in Fountain Street by subscription, 'lighted by elegant chandeliers' and 'resorted to by a numerous assemblage of fair Lancashire witches', according to the Manchester historian Joseph Aston. In Market Square Joseph Harrop, the Tory newspaper proprietor, posted the news in his *Manchester Mercury*. Here everybody could read of business failures and discuss the political news of the day.

The town was dirty, insanitary and crowded, and Joseph Aston remarks on the 'prevalent disposition in so many persons, whose business is carried on in the town, to reside a little way from it, so that the pure breath of heaven may more freely blow upon them'. He also describes the communal grave at St Michaels Church 'where a very large grave, or more properly pit for the reception of mortality, is digged, coffins piled beside and upon each other' – a sinister indication of the death and disease which stalked the townspeople.

But attempts at improvement were continually being made. In 1792 the old exchange was pulled down because it was 'a harbour for vagrants and dirt'. In the same year the new assembly rooms in Mosley Street were built, with a magnificent ballroom, a tea-room, card room and billiard room. On assembly nights the ballroom scintillated with chandeliers and mirrors, the walls had painted panels and the sofas were covered with orange satin. A ten piece orchestra provided the music.

Sarah and William would attend these assemblies, enjoying the fashionable social scene like their contemporaries. Sarah's letters refer to 'high rout time in King Street', so she certainly also attended these private parties or 'routs'. The Manchester friends mentioned in Sarah's letters, like the Simpsons of Hart Hill, the Satterthwaites and the Touchetts, were important and wealthy manufacturers. The young Whittakers moved in the most affluent circles.

When William started his business as a cotton merchant in the 1780s, life in Manchester was exhilarating. It was a boom town, which acted like a magnet for people of enterprise and inventiveness. Business had been stimulated by key inventions to improve the speed and ease of textile manufacture. In 1785 the first steam engine was used in a factory and Edmund Cartwright invented the power loom.

By 1786, the year of William and Sarah's marriage, Manchester was at the beginning of its most meteoric period

Piccadilly, Manchester, in 1790, showing the
infirmary.

of progress, when cotton mills sprang up everywhere and the
population increased dramatically.

Indian cottons had become more modish than silk or linen
for elegant clothes, and the Manchester manufacturers were
rapidly learning how to make their own versions of muslins
and printed calicoes. Cottons could be washed easily, and
thus became popular with fashionable people taking a new
interest in hygiene. The heaviest fustians and velvets for
colder weather could also compete sucessfully with wool,
which seemed clumsy, heavy and countrified to the upwardly
mobile young people of the late eighteenth century.

The cotton business was carried on by merchants who also
sometimes became manufacturers. William Whittaker was
described as 'merchant, dealer and chapman'. They would
undertake anything profitable, becoming dyers, whitsters
(bleachers), drysalters who provided the chemicals for the
industry, calico printers or 'medly' manufacturers. Like the
Yorkshire woolstaplers, they organised the putting out of yarn
to fustian cutters, dyers, whitsters and calendermen all over
the town and in outlying hamlets. They organised the credit
for the operations and supplied the warehouses with finished

products. They were importers and exporters, closely linked with the ports, especially Liverpool.

Connections between Manchester and Liverpool had been greatly improved by the new canal system, and the Mersey and Irwell Canal was eventually extended to Runcorn by the aristocratic canal builder, the Duke of Bridgewater.

In 1788 a serious depression was caused in Manchester because of the large imports of fine muslins from India to meet the insatiable demand. The Manchester manufacturers desperately needed a better supply of good quality 'cotton wool' (raw cotton), and their traditional sources, the West Indies, India and South America, were proving inadequate. For the first time they began to seek supplies from the newly independent United States.

Private banks were established in 1788 and, as coin was scarce, the cotton business used bills of exchange, drafts, and acceptances as currency. It was a dangerous time financially. The difficulty of getting coins, even for wages, meant that most business was carried on with paper. Debts could even be sold as a form of currency. The web of debt

Manchester in 1797.

would often engulf not only businesses but friends and families, including widows and spinsters, from whom entrepreneurs frequently raised their capital.

Although business progressed erratically, with boom and depression in turn, by 1794 Manchester had grown into a town of over 60,000 inhabitants, of whom 20,000 men, women and children were employed in the preparing of warp and weft alone, and 'that takes no account of the weavers, mechanics and domestic servants'.

The 'manufactures of the town', said the *Directory* proudly, 'have now after progressive improvements acquired such celebrity both in the scale of ornament and utility as to spread ten thousand forms and colours, not only in these kingdoms but all over Europe and even into the distant continents'.

William and Sarah had seven years of married life in Manchester before disaster struck them. During that period they naturally wrote no letters to each other, for happily married couples living together have no need to put pen to paper.

Late in 1793, however, there were ominous developments. William's business was in serious difficulties and a financial storm was gathering round his head. Anxious to spare Sarah his worries, in January 1794 he dispatched her and the two children back to the safety of Townhill.

Midwinter was a curious time for such a trip across the Pennines, and Sarah had to leave at the height of the party season in Manchester. Tongues would certainly wag, both in Manchester and Bradford. Sarah was puzzled, anxious and disappointed. She did not fully understand the situation, because William refused to tell her the extent of his problems. All she could do was to write long and amusing letters to cheer up her husband, the lonely 'lord of Brown Street' — and talk hopefully about her return.

Her stepmother Caroline Duffield and her husband Francis may not have welcomed Sarah and the two children with total delight. They perhaps discussed behind her back the reasons for the unexpected winter visit. She was the heiress of

Townhill – might she want to come and live there permanently with her family? It was not a prospect that gave them much pleasure.

To Francis Duffield, Sarah represented a threat to the position he had built up as one of Bradford's leading citizens. He had married his wealthy partner's widow, and he and his wife had already become known as 'the Duffields of Townhill House'.

In the meantime, however, Sarah was glad of their hospitality in her old home. She settled down to write one Sunday afternoon in January 1794, wistful and somewhat embarrassed about her position. Nobody outside the family had been told yet of her arrival, and she was not keen to be seen. She had lain in bed late, on a stormy, cold January morning, leaving baby Sarah to be looked after by the Townhill servants. She sat in her old room and wrote to William:

> Our arrival here last night was too late to allow of writing by the post or my Dr W's request wd. not have been neglected – Our journey was not remarkable for anything, but very rough hard roads which have almost taken away my hoarseness for (without any presbyterianism) it is much better for my Journey and in a few days I don't doubt being able to sing as delightfully as ever, and according to the prophet Daniel [William's brother] 'astonish the natives' – I called upon Mr Buck of Halifax [Sarah's uncle] and found him uncommonly well and was receivd with much rejoicing.

The sensation of being back in her old home without her husband was odd, and her little half-brother was obviously confused by her arrival. She went on:

> Johnny says he almost forgets I'm married now and it will be well if I don't for here I am quite in status quo inhabiting my old apartment and now writing in it upon the very Table wch I used to pen my spinsterly answers

to yr Billet Doux and not a House tree or Wall that I see from my window but looks like an old friend or acquaintance at least – as to my living acquaintance in this neighbourhood (whom I value less than the abovementioned dumb inoffensive ones) I have seen none, nor is my visit made public yet – Farewell my dr Willm . . . and believe me most truly yours S. Whittaker

It was necessary the following week to face the ordeal of going to chapel and the local gossip which would surround her appearance. The Buck family, like many manufacturers and business people, attended the Unitarian chapel, which was within walking distance of Townhill. Unitarianism laid emphasis on practical morality, uprightness, industriousness and charity – excellent tenets for those engaged in business. Sarah hastened to write on her return:

I have been so tossed and blustered about by a very windy walk from chapel that you must expect my letter will consist of many airy flights, but first let me say how highly delighted I am with the eagerness you expressed for my sweet company to town – well then my dear spouse I have considered about it seriously and I find you will be better without me as your stay will be so short and you do not seem much disposed to travel with a clog to your foot, and besides I should feel somewhat indignant to travel in that capacity – therefore I will contentedly remain here till you travel homewards –

William's invitation to her to join him in a trip to London must have been half-hearted to say the least. It was more likely an attempt to raise money than a social visit. Later he also asked her to find out about insurance, and Sarah reported that 'Mr Duffield does not advise it for more than £1000 and if you like will have it included in his Policy'.

There are only these vague and fleeting echoes of William's plight as his wife replied to his letters, which do not survive. He was still succeeding in keeping the extent of his problems a secret from her.

Sarah soon found herself drawn into the social life of Caroline and her friends. Caroline and Francis Duffield had already become patrons of culture. Francis's name appears as a subscriber to the new organ which was built in the parish church in 1784, and he also appeared as a member of the first committee of the Bradford Subscription Library founded in 1774. Among the early subscribers to this library was the Reverend Patrick Brontë.

Among leading Bradford citizens were Sarah's cousin Dawson Humble, the woolstapler, and his wife Hannah. Mr Benjamin Rawson and his family lived at Manor Hall in Kirkgate. Joseph Priestley, the manager of the new Leeds-Liverpool Canal, and his family lived at Stott Hill House near the parish church, and Miss Priestley was a friend of both Caroline and Sarah. Bradford society was small and select, and Townhill parties were prized in the social calendar.

Caroline decided to hold some entertainments and Sarah was forced to face her Bradford friends without her husband. She told William all about it:

> . . . my mother [Caroline Duffield] has sent out near 60 cards for her rout tomorrow – tonight a select audience will assemble for sacred music – during our musical rehearsal for Wednesday Mrs D has engaged several performers from Halifax – the vocalists will be B Slater, Miss Stovin and Mr Mann, who sings a good second, and I expect much greater pleasure from the performance than any of our Manchester concerts afford.

Sarah repeatedly urged William to join her at Townhill:

> . . . if it was convenient for you to reach Littleborough on Tuesday evening you would arrive in good time here – you will not understand from the above that I wish to dictate to my lord and master. I only wish to sketch out a plan which will convey him to much harmony and Sarah

Caroline also sent a coquettish invitation to the musical

An evening assembly at Vauxhall Gardens, London.

evening via Sarah to William's brother Daniel, but '. . . she says she does not think any of our Bradford ladies will go down after the Manchester belles'.

An enthusiastic denial was obviously expected. Sarah wrote on with domestic details and sidelights on many topics:

> I have this moment receivd a letter from Martha Bischoff with a very pressing invitation to Meredith's benefit Concert the 8th of March, it is heard the poor little Archbischoff is in a consumption – you will find in the middle sideboard drawer an abridgement of the history of the New Testament which pray bring over for Johnny – Mr Fox says the young men at Mr Hannam's academy are reckoned wild – he says for learning the languages a private house would be preferable there being many English at the school who associate together adieu my dear William truly your own Sally.

The singers from Halifax who came to take part in the musical evenings organised at Townhill were representatives of a town with a great musical reputation. It was thought to be the most musical place for its size in the kingdom. Glee clubs, musical societies and amateur concerts were numerous. Singing was just as popular among the weavers and spinners and their families, however humble their position. Bradford was quite able to hold its own in the musical sphere, however. Regular 'oratorios', consisting at that time of a variety of items of sacred music, though chiefly the works of Handel, were held in the parish church. 'Concertos' were also held in the assembly room above the new market hall which was built in 1794. A programme for one of these which survives details music for flute, violin and 'grand pianoforte'.

Sarah's description of an oratorio performance she attended is amusingly frank, and we can imagine her fastidious little nose wrinkling:

> On Tuesday evening we attended the performance of Judas Maccabeus. It is a very fine oratorio and there were some very decent performances that upon the whole I was vastly pleased, saving the wonderful heat and perfume arising from a Very Heterogeneous audience (One of whom came with a Sack upon his back), and some very curious figures and countenances as I ever beheld – Upon the whole we had a very merry evening, being luckily near the Door and next to Mrs Dean, who you know is an excellent one for encouraging and partaking of a Laugh . . .

Relentlessly the winter season continued, with routs, concerts, and suppers at all the best Bradford homes. Manchester friends arranged to visit the Bradford assembly in a party. Sarah confided to William that she felt there was something curiously missing in Bradford routs:

> This morning Jack was saddled, Mr. D. [Duffield] booted and myself habited for a ride to Calverley, but rain prevented us – We are now (Jack excepted)

caparisoned for attending a Concert at Mrs Haling's this evening, whch will be succeeded by a Supper – Tomorrow we meet Miss Slater for a party of Bradford Belles at Miss Priestley's – The routs here are in a different style to those at M [Manchester] – and inconvenient to those who are troubld with a Carniv'rous appetite, sometimes continuing till 2 or 3 o'clock when the Guests take themselves Supperless away – but this is *entrenous*, as it only happens occasionally.

Poor Sarah's spirits often failed her, and she hoped and planned continually for her return to Manchester. Meanwhile she wrote letters, arranged visits, enjoyed their musical evenings, and indulged in wishful thinking:

I thank my kind Spouse for his Indulgence in limiting my stay here to my own wishes – it shall not be abused. I long for tidings of a nice nag being purchased, but pray consult Mr. Winter in compassion for my neck – When I see you we will talk about a method of return, the time & c – The evening went off very well last night, Mr Speight excels greatly on the Harpsichord, Miss B Slater was our vocal performer – We are to have a Grand Concert when Miss Stovin arrives – These sort of performances wd I think please you –

Looking over the pages she had written, Sarah apologised, quite unnecessarily, for her letters were probably the only cheerful events in William's life:

I shall have overwhelmed you with scribble – Pardon my pen's loquacity or take yr revenge by a return in kind – and being now a solitary individual, you have time enough to spare for your absent Sarah – who was much pleased by the length of the last she receivd – Adieu dr W – most truly yours – Mr and Mrs D. send their *Congees* wch pray don't forget in return.

When the weather improved, Sarah and Caroline rode to

57

Calverley, with Mrs Duffield riding her new horse, and Sarah gingerly mounted on her brother's pony. Riding was never her strong point:

> We rode yesterday to Calverley, and by that means missed seeing IW [a Whittaker relative] on his return whch I was sorry for – he will I am sure give you a good account of our Baby – Sarah yesterday cut an upper Tooth and apparently with great ease – she has been perfectly well ever since she came –
> Mrs D has just purchased a pad wch she mounted for the first time yesterday – its a very fine creature and pleasant to ride, but I shoud think it too frolicsome after riding sedate lady Camilla – indeed I am become a coward and I felt some fear upon J.B.'s little Titmouse, alias The Bear.

Calverley Vicarage was still a pleasant destination, and both Caroline and Sarah found good company there as they had always done since their youth. Mrs Traviss, Caroline's mother, by now old and frail, lived with the Fabers:

> We found Mrs Traviss better – she had been out in the carriage and seemed very cheerful and comfortable . . . her faculties are much impaird – but her affectionate and polite attention to those about her are inherent and will continue as long as she lives – Mrs Faber was walking in the woods with her son Stanley when we joind them for a sweet romantic Ramble and concluded the Evening with a ride home by Moonlight . . . you give a dreadful account of our Pigstye and Turkies, but I hope better success with our Guineafowls. Mrs D wishes for some much – I believe Mrs. D will undertake to convey 2 live ones to Townhill –

The news from their farm at Moss Side was bad, but very likely William had no time to attend to his livestock, or perhaps he had already been forced to dismiss his farm servants. But he wrote encouraging letters to Sarah, pleading

Part of a letter from Sarah Whittaker to her husband
William Whittaker, 1794.

for the entertainment her lively style of writing gave him, and
she was only too pleased to respond:

> I receivd your Letter my dear William this afternoon
> and as you see make haste to return you one of my
> 'enlivening Scrawls' by way of *douceur* for the tardiness
> of my last whose contents wd. inform you why it was
> delayd, it was not meant as revenge for the saucy
> indifference you was pleased to assume – for I knew that
> was 'all my Eye and Betty Martin' – as I perhaps love
> writing to you as well as you do receiving my Letters.
>
> As proof of the above, Mr Double W, know that I
> have this moment absconded from a Whist party
> consisting of my revd. host, his lively dame, a fine red-
> and-white looking lass his niece and the revd and
> sagacious Mr Haworth, pedagogue and Curate of the
> place, and all this to have a little paper chat with the
> half-widowd, half Bachelor Lord of Brown Street, whose

The Card Party (1783).

situation is truly lamentable being neither one thing nor
the other, and I begin to feel some kind of compunction
for his disconsolate situation and some time in the week
after next he will probably receive all his cares again in
the shape of a Wife! – by that time I think the weather
will have settled enough for me to come Home on a nag.

I had hoped that Mr and Mrs F [Faber] wd have

returned with me but those agreeable hopes are all quashed by the arrival of the above-mentioned Cherry-Cheekd dame — apropos of Cherry Cheeks I am taking great pains with mine and hope to bring a little Yorkshire air in them to Manchester — I gallop for it upon the terrace every day for an Hour or two, imbibing the fresh Breeze with as much avidity and much more advantage than Don Gaskell does with his spirituous potations — all this Day has been devoted to walking Mr F. and Mrs Traviss went to Leeds so Mrs F. and I spent the morning in these heavenly woods under a pure and serene sky and all the afternoon upon the terrace, so its no wonder my faculties are so bright and witty this evening.

Tomorrow Mama dines here and I return with her and on Friday the same party dine at Townhill — where Miss Stovin will join us in the evening — you don't say whether you purchased the house mentioned in your last — now the fine weather comes I am afraid I shall be plaguing you to Death about one — the Day I propose returning home is next Friday fortnight if my Dr W. will please to come and fetch his runaway and Borrow either Lady Camilla or the all-devouring Famine to convey her —

Although Sarah was trying to enjoy the fresh air and country walks, she was clearly anxious about their Manchester home and refers rather wistfully to the party season in Manchester, which she was missing. The restlessness of a young woman used to more sophisticated amusements is obvious as she contemplates the dubious joys of playing draughts with the elderly Mrs Traviss:

I fancy this is high rout time in King Street — well poor little gay souls I don't envy them, unless indeed Mrs Traviss shd summon me to a game at Drafts which is a sport if anything *rather less delectable* than Commerce or Vingt Une — tell me of whom the Assembly

party will consist – Goodnight! and pray write soon to
yr. little 'Dog's Face'

William's latest excuse for not coming to Bradford was his
father's sudden illness. Sarah began to cancel her visiting
plans, hoping that this crisis would make her return to
Manchester essential:

I recd. your Letter last night just as the Concert was
commencing and was very much shocked with the
business. . . You wd. all be vastly alarmd – I had no
thought of prolonging my stay beyond tomorrow sennight
[week] or sooner if you wish it or if my Father [Mr
Whittaker senior] is worse. I have written this morning
to decline Miss Bischoff's invitation, telling her my
continuance here is very uncertain.

Our concert last night went off very well about 12
performers and the same number of auditors it began at
4 and concluded at ½ past one –

In spite of all the complicated plans, Sarah's arrangements
were turned upside down again:

Sunday noon
A Total revolution in my plans dr Wm. is occasioned
by some Letters this morning one to inform me that the
Mr Simpsons are at Bath and another whch obliges Mr
Duffield to take a sudden journey to London and he
proposes going on Tuesday. I am therefore going to
Calverley this afternoon and shall return on Wed
morning, by which means Mrs. D will not be left much
alone – Miss S[Stovin] will be here about Saturday and
the beginning of next week is devoted to some merry
parties wch I am old-fashioned enough to wish my
Husband coud conveniently join – Friday in the same
week is the last Assemblies – I hope to find a Letter
when I return on Wednesday – This little Billet will

serve as a contrast to the last – Enter dinner and farewell spouse – Ever yrs.

Sarah the Hungry.

Sarah's signature was only half a joke. The parting was trying her patience, and she was hungry not only for dinner but for the arms of her dear William.

With Trembling Hand and Aching Heart

William's bankruptcy, 1794

William Whittaker was facing the collapse of his business in Manchester. The cause of his downfall is not discoverable, but it could have been simply lack of business prudence, or working too much on credit in the unsettled business conditions of 1793. There is a good deal of discussion in the letters about the proceeds of an insurance claim, which may point to the possibility that William's goods had been lost at sea. It seems likely that he was engaged in exporting, or perhaps had been advanced the money for the import of raw cotton which failed to arrive.

William's business failure occurred during a dangerous and difficult time. The period 1789 to 1793 was full of new problems for commerce. The French Revolution upset trade with Europe, and by 1793 relations with the revolutionary government had deteriorated so much that war broke out between Britain and France. The war went badly at first for the British. There were horrific losses in Flanders and in the West Indian swamps where the troops died in thousands from fever.

Bankruptcies trebled because of the interruption of trade caused by the war, and there was a good deal of commercial distress. Men enlisted in the army as much because of the depression as out of patriotism. The Manchester manufacturers had to give food and help to their distressed workers, and noted bitterly that London did not seem to have the same problems as the North.

Manchester newspapers were full of bankruptcy notices

and letters on the sorry state of trade from acutely anxious businessmen. Firms failed daily, and half Manchester was thought to be insolvent. Many desperate debtors looked longingly towards America as a possible escape route, and tried to muster enough money from family and friends to set them up as farmers in the New World.

On the 29th January 1794, Aunt Todd in London replied to a letter from Sarah which does not survive. The worldly-wise Todds had been expecting bad news. Not for the first time, Aunt Todd's meticulous heading of her letters proves invaluable in unravelling the story, as it dated William's public disgrace precisely.

> With Trembling Hand and Aching Heart have I perused and re-perused my Dear very Dear Mrs Whittaker's Letter just receiv'd – we have for some time past had an Alarming Apprehension and scarce Entertained a Glimmering Hope that all was right – yet I must confess though in some degree prepared for it, yet the Confirmation this morning proved Exceedingly Painfull.

Aunt Todd urgently reminded Sarah of the 'Serious and Interesting Conversation' her Uncle Stephen had felt obliged to have with her the previous summer at Wither. Luckily Sarah, although a loyal and loving wife, did take the advice to heart, and managed to keep her head enough to hold on to her own useful fortune. Her trustees had ensured that she would be financially independent of her husband in the event of any business failure, and she was prudent enough not to try to vary this provision. Aunt Todd warned her again:

> . . . not upon any Consideration whatever to relinquish – but hold sacred – everything you either have in present possession or in certain Reversion – and how happy and thankful we ought to be, my dear Mrs Whittaker that, with Frugal Oeconomy Comfortable Bread for you and yours is Secured.

In spite of her 'Pen being Tardy upon the Unpleasing

Part of a letter from Aunt Todd to her niece
Sarah Whittaker, 1794.

Subject', Aunt Todd succeeded in composing several sentences of philosophical reflection:

> Life may well be called a Warfare, a Mixture of good
> and ill, and to submit calmly to Tryalls such as the
> present, requires all Human Exertion – your Reason and
> Religion I Dispair not will come to your aid – God grant
> you his support –

Uncle Stephen Todd, a solidly prosperous businessman,

no doubt shook his head over his nephew-in-law's troubles. But hovering at his wife's shoulder, he offered his own support:

> Mr Todd bids me say you may rely on his Affectionate regard and steady continued freindship – He is not a Fickle Being and many have been his mortifications through the Varied Scenes of Life, which Experience, with Tenderness makes him feel the Sufferings of others . . . do, my dear Mrs Whittaker, keep up your Spirits – let your Little Folks both delight and amuse you – what Comforts may be in store you know not – I shall be glad to be Acquainted with Mr Whittaker's intended Plan of proceeding – what is painfull relate not –

The disasters befalling the Whittaker family had begun before Christmas 1793. On the 23rd December William's house in Brown Street was let by auction at the Bulls Head. The advertisement of this sale in the *Manchester Mercury* was the first newspaper report of the collapse of the Whittaker family's fortunes.

Daniel Whittaker, a 'check and muslin manufacturer', and probably William's father, was next to lose his house in King Street. A week earlier he had assigned all his real and personal estate in trust for the benefit of his creditors. Soon after Christmas there were further shocks. On the 4th January Daniel's horses were sold, and on the 4th February his house at Higher Lane, Pilkington, with its 'warping mills, yarn boxes and cotton, good lights, two good hot beds and glasses and a choice collection of greenhouse plants'. The day before, the household contents and livestock – cows, carts and farming utensils – were auctioned.

On the 5th February, Mr Walker the auctioneer announced the dispersal of 'all the elegant Household Furniture, plate, linen, China, glassware, brewing vessels, two horses and two cows and a quantity of good hay, and all the extensive hot houses, garden glasses etc together with the farming stock at the house of Mr William Whittaker at Moss Side in the township of Hulme near the barracks'. On the 7th, he announced, would 'begin to be sold by auction All the stock in trade of the said Mr Whittaker at his warehouse in Marsden Street'.

These announcements date the Whittakers' public humiliation, and finally brought the disaster cruelly home to Sarah.

William's bankruptcy notice was posted in the *Manchester Mercury* on the 18th and 24th March 1794. 'William Whittaker, merchant, dealer and chapman', was required to 'surrender himself to the Commissioners in Bankruptcy on the thirteenth and fourteenth of March and the twelfth day of April following to make a full discovery and disclosure of his estate and Effects'.

We hear nothing further of the elder Whittaker, but William's sisters lost their inheritance in the crash, as was usual in those times when people raised capital from their mothers, fathers, sisters and brothers. William's brother Daniel assumed responsibility for them.

William's downfall brought him powerful enemies. His principal creditor, Thomas Tipping, was a younger son of a distinguished Lancashire family. The senior Tipping branch, headed by a baronet, had large estates in Buckinghamshire and Oxfordshire. The younger branch moved to Manchester and became involved in the cotton business. Thomas Tipping was born in 1747, and at the time of William's bankruptcy was a well-known and affluent cotton merchant. His country home was at the fashionable and exclusive Ardwick Green, then a pleasant country village.

Aunt Todd was horrified to hear of the extent of the disaster, and wrote that 'The situation of those at Ardwick is truly lamentable, and the whole of the family being involved dreadful –'

The dismay and rage of the 'family at Ardwick', drawn into the whirlpool of William's collapse, was indeed to prove crucial to William and Sarah's future. The Tippings were already planning to take their revenge in full.

Thomas Tipping had been a partner in the firm of Peel,

Yates, Tipping and Halliwell – not a firm to be trifled with, as the Whittakers were to discover to their cost. A possible scenario for William's downfall is that he had been advanced the money for the import of raw cotton for Thomas Tipping, and the consignment had been lost at sea. For an obscure merchant like William Whittaker, a connection with these eminent manufacturers must have been a sign of business progress, and perhaps he had risked more than was prudent on their behalf.

Tipping owned warehouse property in Tippings Court in Cannon Street, a cheap green-field site at that time, and far from Manchester's commercial centre. The celebrated cotton tycoon Robert Peel had rented Tipping's warehouse, no doubt for reasons of economy, and took him into partnership. The effect of the dynamic Peel on the Cannon Street area was to be remarkable – within twenty-five years it became full of manufacturers' and merchants' houses, often with their warehouses attached.

But in 1794, Peel was already a major figure in the cotton trade. His nickname was 'Parsley Peel', because a best-selling design in his printed fabrics was a parsley leaf. His business was originally calico printing, but he later undertook a complete 'vertical' operation, imported cotton, spun and wove it, bleached and printed it, and finally exported the finished fabric. Robert Peel married the daughter of his partner, Mr Yates, and when he died left the remarkable fortune of £2,000,000.

Mr Peel, Mr Yates and Mr Halliwell were a powerful combination. Their partner Thomas Tipping was an equally formidable figure.

Sarah was immensely anxious following the public disclosure of William's financial troubles and the the sale of all her household possessions. She consulted all the men in the family. Francis Duffield was thoroughly *au fait* with the prospects for debtors, and no doubt was in the habit of enlarging at the Townhill dinner table on the arguments in favour of a recent relaxation of the law.

Previously to the Debtors Act of 1793, people could be imprisoned for three months when they owed as little as four shillings. This meant that they had no hope at all of earning the money to pay their debts, or in fact of ever escaping from the debtor's jail. In evidence for the new act it was stated that in the Bradford debtors' prison 'there languished fifteen persons, the parents of seventy-three children, owing only seventeen pounds between them'.

Francis Duffield was one of forty-eight respectable persons ('all that there were in Bradford at this time', says John James, the Bradford historian), appointed commissioners in the Court of Requests of Bradford to administer the new law. It was still severe: the penalty for debts of up to forty shillings was forty days; and twenty shillings, twenty days.

The commissioners, who had to possess £500 in personal wealth or £20 per year in property, also included Sarah's cousin Dawson Humble, Edmund Peckover the Quaker banker, Joseph Priestley the Leeds and Liverpool Canal manager, and Abraham Balme, the stone merchant who had been a private banker to her father.

Although debtors with some standing or influence, able to summon help from their families and friends, could often buy their way out of the worst of the prison conditions, the fear of a debtor's jail amounted almost to paranoia.

If small debtors could expect such harsh punishment, what could William expect, owing thousands of pounds? The bankruptcy might not suffice to protect him, and Sarah feared that it was only a matter of time before an enraged creditor, probably Thomas Tipping, saw to it that her husband was thrown into prison as a debtor, probably never to emerge.

Advice flooded in from the family, and in March 1794, Sarah made a trip to Manchester, for an anxious consultation with her husband. Aunt Todd wrote to her niece, glad that after an 'Agreeable Journey' Sarah had:

> a safe arrival at Townhill and a happy ending with your Little Folks – and so affectionate and freindly a

reception from Mr and Mrs Duffield – I must confess how great was my mortification that your last was so much out of Spirits anticipating Evills and fearing Dreadful Consequences – which Mr Todd is clearly of Opinion only exist in your Imagination

Mr Todd was of a brisk and sensible turn of mind, and his views were forthright. Aunt Todd relayed them carefully, her pen scratching laboriously across the pages as he dictated:

Mr Todd cannot possibly think otherwise, that if upon Close Examination Mr Whittaker renders a fair and candid account before the Assignees and Creditors – and gives up all – how can he be further Punishable? – and when things are Settled must be so far Acquitted as to be at Liberty –

The question Stephen Todd asked so bluntly must have occurred to everyone. Why indeed did William fear his creditors so much?

'Sometimes in cases such as this', continued Aunt Todd optimistically, 'people are at first irritated – and when cooler Reflection takes place we frequently find Resentment subside and kind consideration for so Worthy a Distressed Family will powerfully Work upon Reason and Conscience –'

Stephen Todd wanted to allay Sarah's fears for William's liberty and her forebodings for the future:

Mr Todd cannot entertain any other Expectation but Mr Whittaker will be at Liberty – there are Instances thousands upon thousands who are free and no Certificate signed – shoud Mr Whittaker ever by fortunate chance get into a Situation where he might have the Opportunity of Realising Property, he might be called upon with Justice in the Claim – but at present Mr Todd cannot think there will be any Danger of an Arrest – for anybody to tell you a Sepparation for you is necessary from Mr Whittaker or your children is an absurdity indeed –

71

Exhorting Sarah to trust in God – 'his power Uncontrollable and mercy Infinite' – Aunt Todd fervently hoped that the crucial personalities in the case were being succoured:

> . . . am glad indeed that the Ardwick family has so many freinds by whose Efforts of Assistance they have a prospect of getting Comfortable Bread – Afluance is not requisite for happiness and Content is great Riches –

In spite of reassurance, William and Sarah both remained uneasy, and eventually family assistance was invoked in a practical plan to remove him from the wrath of his creditors. It was decided that he would ride to London and take discreet lodgings where he would arrange to join a ship for America. Sarah sent some of her own money to the Todds to help eke out William's modest funds. Mr Todd volunteered to go and find his nephew-in-law and pass on the welcome banknote.

Unlike his wife, Stephen Todd did not indulge in pious hopes and elaborate phraseology. Nor did he like wasting money. What he thought of William's financial acumen, courage and even honesty, is not made plain. But he did the job, for his niece's sake, and wrote to Sarah on the 13th June 1794:

> My dear Mrs Whittaker's letter with a bill enclosed forty pounds came safe to hand Tuesday last – and agreeable to your request I went immediately in pursuit of Mr Whittaker and soon found where he was – I acquainted him with the contents of your letters and my commission which I found was very acceptable – as his money was nearly exhausted and was in want of several little things – I desird he woud make me out an account of what he wanted to make him comfortable on his voyage and also that he might have a little supply of money with him upon his arrival – and bring it to me yesterday to dinner which he did – and after looking over it and putting things together we agreed that thirty pounds woud amply supply his wants and leave him 15

or 16£ in money. That sum I have given him today –
and the remaining 10£ I have paid to Messrs Castell and
Co on Mr Duffield's account –

One can visualise the meeting at the Todds' house. What
William's thoughts were as Mr Todd totted up his requirements, decided that £30 was enough and sent the rest back
to Sarah, is not recorded. Mr Todd's firm and commanding
handwriting makes it clear that one did not argue with him.
Nor did he mince words:

> You say the examinations of Mr Whittaker is closed
> – and that he has left Manchester 'in safety' which
> implies a fear of his creditors – I have not heard how
> he has made up the account to justify himself therefore
> I am unable to give my opinion of his future prospects –

Although Stephen Todd took a cool, crisp view of the
affair, in the loyal and possibly prejudiced eyes of Sarah and
William's brother Daniel, Thomas Tipping was the biggest
ogre in Manchester. He certainly had cause to be severely
provoked by 'the loss of his thousands', as Daniel airily
described it later – which represented an immense sum in
the 1790s. His threats were enough to engineer the hapless
William's terrified flight, which may have given him at least
some grim satisfaction.

Aunt Todd's next letter to Sarah in December 1794
describes an encounter on the way to London as the Todds
bowled down the Great North Road in their carriage. Her
description of a tragic family was probably intended to
remind her niece that at least Sarah's troubles were only
pecuniary:

> . . . we had a safe journey tho' a tedious one only
> arriving in Leadenhall street yesterday about half-past
> one o'clock – Accidentally Mr Todd see the Waggon
> which conveyed the Affectionate Afflicted father – along
> with his Darling Child – to that Asylum where the

Divine Blessing I hope may prove Effectual to a happy restorative to Reason and rational Comfort – she was strongly Affected at seeing me – her Spirits greatly disturbed – and repeatedly calld out 'Oh Mrs Todd – I never in all my life designed to do anybody any harm' – her idea was she was going to Prison as a place of punishment – a Moving Scene – may God relieve her mind – the Good Old man stays a day or two with us – astonishingly submissive and says the last Night's refreshing sleep has composed his Thoughts to resignation and beleives it Good to be Afflicted . . . to your little Sarah all my love and William if he forget me will I hope remember the promise of more Biscuits from Aunt Todd.

This was kind Aunt Todd's last letter to Sarah, and she died in 1795. Uncle Stephen wrote to Sarah sadly:

my loss is irreperable – My dearest wife is only gone a little before me – it cannot in the course of nature be long before I follow – and I fervently pray that I may be as well prepared for the dreadful summons when it arrives . . .

The estimable lady had left her niece some practical help, explained Mr Todd:

Her anxious solicitude for you was great indeed – she has not forgot that you wanted aid after she was no more – and that you may be in possession of it immediately I have purchased £625 of 4% Annuity at 80 per cent which is the 500£ she left you and put it into the names of Dawson Humble and Joseph Wright the trustees appointed by her Will. This will produce you an income of 25£ per annum during your life and the principal for your children after your death.

Even Aunt Todd's legacy was carefully put into the hands of suitable male trustees. It was the custom of the time, for which Sarah already had reason to be thankful. Women whose capital was not carefully tied up could as easily fall victim to the bankruptcy of their husbands and other relatives as they could to fortune-hunters and unscrupulous heart-breakers.

300 sail and a fair wind

The Liverpool connection, 1794-1795

The plan of action to help William Whittaker involved Michael Humble, a wealthy Liverpool merchant and a relative of the Humble branch of the family. He was an important family connection at Idle near Bradford, his wife being Harriet Hird, the daughter of a local landowner. He travelled regularly to Liverpool where he had his business. Like Mr Todd, Mr Humble could not resist an appeal from the attractive Mrs Whittaker. He was persuaded, probably through family pressure, that William should become a cotton buyer in the American South for the Humble enterprise, and that he should set out for Charleston, South Carolina, as soon as possible. Funds were to be provided by arrangement with Mr Humble and Mr Todd.

Once the summer season had passed, however, there was no possibility of sailing until the following spring. William spent the winter of 1794 waiting anxiously with friends and relatives in London and Bath, or in the most economical lodgings he could find. The wait for a passage across the Atlantic must have seemed endless, and in fact he did not take ship until the early summer of 1795.

The prosperous and generous Mr Humble lived well and entertained well. During Sarah's enforced stay in Bradford, she reported that 'on Monday we are to eat Turtle at Mr Humble's – one of 200 lb weight is to come ready dressed from Liverpool'. The turtle was a spectacular treat, only possible because of Mr Humble's business in the port. Live turtles were sometimes brought home by seamen to sell. They were kept in tanks during the voyage home.

Mr Humble's firm appears consistently in the Liverpool directories from 1790 to 1810, where 'Michael Humble, merchant', is shown as having been joined by partners Hurry, Holland and Pool. Humble and Hurry were also among the important turn-of-the-century shipbuilders of the flourishing port. Humble and Holland founded a pottery in 1796 and later went over to the manufacture of fine bone china. Renamed 'Herculanaeum' in imitation of Wedgwood's 'Etruria', the firm became famous, and its wares are today highly sought after by collectors. Not everything went smoothly with Mr Humble and his partners, however, and in 1804, Daniel Whittaker, William's brother, who was a Liverpool cotton broker, wrote that 'Mr Humble is detained in Liverpool – a nasty business, a Dissolution of Partners in the house – H.H. and Pool are turned out it is in the Gazette'.

Michael Humble could be opinionated and hasty, as William and Sarah were to find out, but the cause of the quarrel with his partners is not known.

Liverpool merchants at the end of the eighteenth century were confident and proud of their achievements. They could be seen strolling about the elegant new buildings and streets of their well-built town, says Richard Brooke, the mid-Victorian Liverpool historian, in 'court dress coats with stand-up collars, and gilt, silvered twist or basket buttons, waistcoats of very great length called flap waistcoats . . . short breeches with buckles of gold, silver, or false stones at the knee or gilt or plated to resemble those in their shoes. Their coats, waistcoats and breeches were often of one colour, light or snuff. They wore silk stockings, ruffles at the wrist, a white stock for the throat, and carried canes or walking sticks.'

The Liverpool merchants did not see any necessity to alter the successful ways of their predecessors. The port's prosperity dated from the mid-eighteenth century when it began to trade extensively with the West Indies. Its imports of sugar, rum and coffee were increasingly balanced by its

The custom house, St Thomas's Church and the old
dock, Liverpool.

exports of salt and coal, but it also reaped the profits from
its most notorious trade – slaves.

Although the slave trade was controversial long before the
turn of the century, Liverpool people were reluctant to join
the abolitionists. Liverpool seamen thought, probably with
some justification, that their own lives were as hard as those
of the slaves, and maintained that their captains were more
humane to their human cargoes than African kings or Arab
slave-traders. The peak year for the Liverpool slave traders
was 1799, when 134 ships were fitted out for slaving. Goree
Piazza was named after the West African island to which the
slavers went for their cargoes. Branding irons for slaves could
be seen for sale in Liverpool shops.

By the time Michael Humble was in business and
appearing in the Whittaker letters, cotton from the southern
states of America and the West Indies was becoming one of
Liverpool's most important imports. The port was ideally
placed to deal with the voracious demand for raw cotton in
Manchester. Finished cotton goods also went to Liverpool for
export to most countries of the world, including the slave
plantations of the American South.

There were many problems and difficulties associated with American trade, including bad debts, bankruptcies, ships foundering and being captured on the high seas; but Liverpool and Manchester merchants strove to develop this side of their business. The outbreak of war with France in 1793 made the Atlantic crossing even more hazardous, but Liverpool businessmen struggled desperately to keep it going, because their formerly flourishing trade with Europe was cut off.

A major object of British naval policy during the war was to keep the Atlantic open for trade and to hamper the efforts of France to bring supplies from the New World. Admiral Hood's battle of the Glorious First of June in 1794 developed from an attempt to stop a French grain convoy from America reaching the French ports.

The cotton brokers, of whom William's brother Daniel was one, were the 'marketing men' of the industry, catering for the joint needs of the importer of raw cotton and the exporter of finished cotton goods. The broker often dealt in other goods

On the Mersey at Liverpool, with ships in distress.

as well, and was permanently installed at the port with warehouse and storage facilities.

With his family connections in Liverpool, William felt confident that a new chapter in his life was beginning, one which would wipe out his disgrace and rehabilitate him in England. The riches which an enterprising man could make in the New World were a favourite topic eagerly discussed in the coffee houses. The risks and dangers could only be surmounted by men of the strongest and most determined character – could William Whittaker rise to the challenge?

It was with exhilaration that William wrote to Sarah from Tenerife in June 1795. After the tiresomely long wait for a ship, he had finally embarked at Portsmouth and found himself sailing with the West India convoy, a fleet of merchant shipping with a majestic naval escort. To a landlubber, the voyage was itself an adventure, but the sight of this huge fleet and the escorting men of war was even more impressive. He described the events proudly and excitedly:

I wrote to you from Portsmouth about 2 Days before we sailed which you would learn from the Papers was on Sunday the 24th of May now 16 days gone – the Fleet convoy we were told, at least 300 sail and a fair wind which continued till we got clear of the Channel on Tuesday evening, when we were off the Lizard at Pollack which was the last land we saw until we made the Island of Canaria which is within sight of this Island on Sunday morning –

On the Wednesday the Wind increased to a very hard gale which continued increasing till Friday morning the 29th of May when we had company with all the Fleet except about 10 or 12 sail which from their taking different courses some to the east and some to the west we concluded to be part of the ships bound to the Straights of the West Indies, but as each made the best of their way to their destined ports we soon lost sight of the whole – afterwards a ship of war and a brig came in sight when we hoisted the flag which they answered and then made another for us to lay to till they came up with us which they did and hailed us on enquiry after the convoy and when we parted from them we had a safe voyage – they left us to pursue our course which we did till the 4th of June without seeing a single sail.

The 'Fleet convoy' of '300 sail' was certainly a magnificent sight, but the reality of trying to assemble it and organise a safe crossing was appallingly difficult. Most competent seamen were already pressed into the navy and the merchantmen could only call on older men and boys, who were either past their best or too inexperienced. Organising the motley fleet of merchant ships was an awe-inspiring task for the navy, and the delays were infuriating to traders – especially the Northerners, who resented having to wait for London merchants before they could sail. They complained that by the time the convoy was ready they had already lost their oppportunities for seasonal trade to competitors.

Nonetheless, prudence demanded patience, for the insurance companies would not pay out on cargoes lost as a result of being sent across the Atlantic in 'runners' – swift ships which attempted, often successfully, to beat the system, relying on their speed to avoid French privateers.

The brig *Margaret*, William's ship, arrived off Tenerife on the 9th June 1795, and as she attempted to gain a landfall, William had ample time to study the appearance of the island. He felt its strangeness well deserved some traveller's prose:

> As I know you will be anxious to hear from me at the first oppportunity, I begin this off Tenerife where we have been beating against contrary Winds and strong currents since Sunday. But as we have got so near as to have got a Pilot from the Shore we hope to get the Ship Moord in the Morning when we hope to go on Shore.
>
> The appearance of the Land is quite new to me and almost beyond my abilities to describe. The Peak is an

immense Pile – regular like a fine sugar loaf which appears above the Clouds and in clear weather is seen at the amazing distance of 50 or 60 Leagues, but the Land on which it stands is amazing high and in many places perpendicular and rugged Rocks at the foot of which the Sea is unfathomable – along the West side in many places the Land has a very fruitful appearance and the ground rising regularly but very steep to a great height which has been continually covered with Clouds since we came – it is the Top of the Peak only we have seen and that at a distance of about 30 miles –

William was awakened by the captain and told to get ready for disembarkation. A fast brig took the passengers and the captain ashore, where their lodgings had been arranged:

. . . on account of the total want of accommodation except in the merchants' houses where the captain and all passengers are received during the stay of this vessel. I have been very hospitably received and upon the whole have passed my time pleasantly. I had intended giving you a long letter but have had so many papers to copy for Mr Humble respecting business and my remarks upon it as I think something may be done to advantage.

I have been very well since I came here and though the heat is rather great I have not found any inconvenience though the thermometer has been from 75 to 78 – I will write you on the passage very fully from the Barbados or the first Island we make.

I have laid in plenty of vegetables and as we have the trade winds hope to make a short passage – we have no news here except a paper of May 20th with accounts of disturbances at Paris – also in Ireland.

When you write to Charles Town I wish you woud get me a respectable Letter of Introduction. Yrs in haste, truly and affectionately my dear Sarah, WW.

It is interesting to note that as a passenger, William was expected to provide at least some of his own victuals. He understood perfectly well that lack of fresh food could be the principal cause of ill-health on a long voyage.

The naivety of William's last sentence, however, almost takes one's breath away. With over a year in which to plan his expedition, how was it that he set sail without any 'respectable introduction'? Was it possible that Mr Humble expected him to do business in South Carolina without any preparation for his reception? And did he seriously think Sarah could assist him?

The signs were already slightly ominous. William seemed to have had only the vaguest idea of what to expect in the New World. Mr Humble, whose business it was to deal abroad, could scarcely have been as innocent as his emissary.

The *Margaret* landed William at Baltimore. From there he took ship to Charleston, arriving in October 1795. His voyage had taken four months.

my Heart is very full

Charleston, 1795

Charleston, South Carolina, where William sat down in November 1795 to write to Sarah, must have seemed a daunting place. He was short of money, and was clearly very homesick in a prosperous and fashionable foreign city. Far from finding himself in a pioneering atmosphere, William quickly realised that doing business in Charleston would be both difficult and expensive.

Scenes of bustling activity met him as he wandered round the wharves and warehouses of East Bay Street, Charleston's eighteenth century commercial area. Here were the merchants' houses, factors, grocers, ships' chandlers, cotton and rice traders. He watched auction sales of produce, goods and slaves, porters hurrying with huge sacks, cargoes being loaded and unloaded. Ships were constantly arriving and departing at the quays, which were rather ramshackle structures, formed with the trunks of palm trees fixed together and laid in alternate square formation one above the other.

On the open ground floor of the handsome exchange building, merchants would meet to discuss business, and an upper floor was used for assemblies. Next to the exchange stood a coffee house and tavern, in a modest little building which still survives.

The houses now known as Rainbow Row on East Bay Street were typical of those owned by substantial merchants. It is not hard to imagine William Whittaker gazing with envy and frustration at their lighted windows and the comings and goings of scurrying clerks and wealthy visitors in carriages.

Artist's impression of eighteenth century merchants' houses on East Bay Street, Charleston, now known as Rainbow Row.

Charleston had been founded in 1670 when a group of English settlers landed on the low-lying, marshy coast at a spot they called Charles Town in honour of their monarch, Charles II. Harassed by dangerous fevers and the hurricanes which lashed the Carolina coast, the colony nevertheless grew into a thriving seaport on the peninsula of land known as Oyster Point, lying between the Ashley and Cooper Rivers. The port had been attacked and occupied by the British during the American War of Independence, but since the signing of peace in 1783 it had flourished anew.

Ships loaded here with deer skins, lumber and hemp, followed later by rice and indigo, and finally cotton. When they returned across the Atlantic, they brought the staples and luxuries of Europe. Charles Town, prosperous and cosmopolitan, became known as a 'Little London' in the wilds of the new World. English visitors called it 'the most agreeable city in America'. It was spaciously laid out – the earliest example of city grid planning in America, with the 'Great Streets' (now Meeting and Broad) intersecting at Market Square.

By the time William Whittaker arrived in Charleston in search of business, cotton was overtaking rice as the most important crop. The long-stapled, creamy-white, strong, silky fibre of the cotton from Carolina's Sea Islands was in the greatest demand for superior quality cotton fabrics, and it could be produced economically by slave labour on the plantations.

Cotton increased the city's wealth, and Charleston citizens lived graciously, with rich costumes, elegant houses, carriages and many servants. Literature, art and music flourished, and Charlestonians loved race meetings and

Charleston, South Carolina in the 1780s.

86

assemblies. They were also deeply religious, and founded many fine churches.

When George Washington visited the city in 1791 he found it 'wealthy, gay and hospitable' and was enchanted by its fashionable, beautiful, witty ladies. Four hundred of them graced a fine concert at the exchange in his honour – 'the number and appearance of which exceeded anything of the kind I had ever seen', remarked the father of his country appreciatively.

Charleston men were independent and frank, but were charged with 'haughty' and 'supercilious' behaviour, said John Drayton, the Governor of South Carolina at this period. Other visitors reported that the Charleston men were idle and dissipated, giving the mornings entirely to billiards and the evenings to 'segars' and debauchery. Governor Drayton also disapprovingly noted 'lately, a flood of dissipation and extravagance'.

George Washington also climbed the steeple of St Michaels Church to view the city, and estimated its inhabitants as 'sixteen thousand souls, about 8000 of them white'. The streets were unpaved, sandy and strewn with oyster shells, but the houses were substantially built of brick and wood, mostly the latter. Ten years later, François Michaux, a French observer of Charleston life, reported that the streets were wide but still not paved. 'Consequently', he said, 'every time your foot slips from a kind of brick pavement before the doors, you are immerged nearly ancle-deep [sic] in sand.'

William Whittaker did not know how to break into the charmed circle of Charleston life. His immensely lengthy letter made poor Sarah's heart sink. The anxious months since his departure had seemed like an age, but she had written so many letters and thought about him continually. Yet he had apparently received not a single word from her.

When she received this description of his isolation and depression, she must have wept tears of frustration. He headed his letter 'Charleston S.Ca. Nov 14 1795':

Artist's impression of St Michaels Church, Charleston.

I know not how to begin this Letter to you my dearest Sarah for my Heart is very full. It has pleased the Almighty to give me good and even nay great spirits as well as very good health since I left you, always

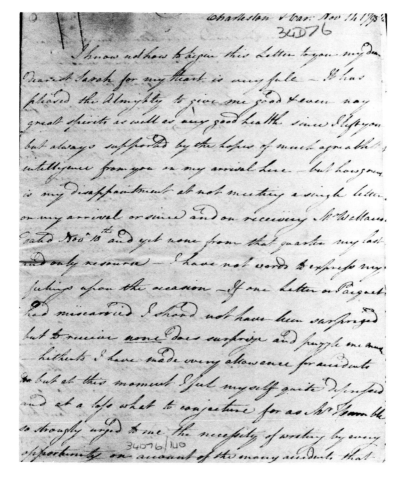

Part of a letter from William Whittaker to his wife
Sarah Whittaker, 1795.

supported by the hopes of much agreeable intelligence
from you on my arrival here – but how great my
disappointment at not meeting with a single Letter or
Paquet on my arrival or since. I have not words to
express my feelings upon the occasion –
Hitherto I have made every allowance for accidents

but at this moment I feel myself quite dispirited and at a loss what to conjecture for as Mr Humble strongly urged me to the necessity of writing by every opportunity on account of the many accidents that happen in Foreign Correspondence I had no doubt that the same precautions woud have been taken on his part. It is now 6 months since I left England and most of the Ships from London and Liverpool with goods for the Fall Trade are arrived, of which there were at least 10 or 12 from those ports came into Baltimore during my stay there, which of course lessens my chance of getting Letters as there are so few expected before the Spring Trade opens –

William had rapidly realised that his funds were not adequate even for living in Charleston, let alone for establishing himself as an agent. Few English merchants kept establishments in the American states, and in any case he had arrived without suitable business contacts. He had to glean what information he could on business conditions from casual acquaintances.

His worst problem was that having heard nothing from Mr Humble, he had no idea whether to buy cotton or not. This was a common dilemma for the transatlantic traders. Buying and selling were hopelessly inhibited by the lack of market information and the hazards of the war. Prices see-sawed up and down, and there was often either a glut or an extreme shortage of cotton. Shortages would make English merchants seize any opportunities they had to fill their warehouses to overflowing, and the price would then plummet because nobody wanted any more. Only the bold or the careless could act decisively.

William was hesitant, and not unnaturally, since he was living on borrowed money and had recently experienced a business failure. He was anxious to appear prudent:

Living is very high here and I cannot attempt making

many purchases in Cotton situated as I am in the Dark
with regard to all information of the state of the markets
in England – Indeed at present I am not acquainted here
with a Merchant in the place nor anyone except the
Lodgers in the house in which I board – I mentioned to
you formerly that Mr Brown a fellow voyager from
Martinique had introduced me to a Boarding House in
Baltimore, and a very agreeable Society, in doing which
he gave up his Bed the only one at Liberty in the house
to me, and as he was going to England to establish a
correspondence and meant to make Liverpool in his
way, I gave him a letter to Mr Humble –

In the absence of introductions to Charleston society,
William had to live in a typical boarding house, as he had
done when he first arrived in Baltimore. He made the best
of it:

> . . . the House I am now in is kept by a Widow Lady
> and the number of the boarders 7 or 8 and all seem good
> kind of Men and 3 or 4 sensible and agreeable, and one
> of them an Irishman (indeed we are almost all Irish) is
> a very clever sensible man and possesses all that
> generosity and hospitality for which his countrymen are
> eminent –

Sarah, Mr Todd and Michael Humble had no doubt
impressed on William the absolute necessity of keeping a
very close account of his expenditure, which he was trying
faithfully to do, as he explained:

> here I must Observe that in my last to you I mentioned
> my intention of proceeding to Savannah, but I coud not
> go but at considerable Expence there being no mode by
> land but to buy a Horse which are very dear and a great
> Expence to keep, and they ask 15$ to 20$ a Day for the
> Hire besides Keep, and by Sea if I had to return woud
> have been 30 dollars at least. Money goes no way here

91

– mine is all expended, it hardly brought me here for the passage money from Baltimore exclusive of Liquors was 38 dollars (inclosed). I have sent you a copy of my expenditure since I left England by which you will see that the Cash of £50 with the Profits makes £80 and sent Capt Hall £20 and expended £60 makes the gross statement of the account.

Since his arrival in Charleston, he had been puzzled by the pattern of seasonal activity. In the early autumn the city had been quiet and deserted almost to the point of paralysis. William was alarmed to discover that so great were the dangers of fever in the summer months that people avoided social contact, and it was thought to be fatal for a white man to spend a night on a plantation. Wealthy people would travel abroad, to the north or to the outlying Sea Islands, at the beginning of the summer, to escape the contagion, when Charleston became a 'melancholy' and 'sickly' place.

But by mid-November, when his first surviving letter was written, a miraculous change had taken place. Social and business life flourished through the winter, when plays and concerts, race meetings and parties were all held and all the planters came to live in their town houses.

François Michaux also described the beginning of the active season thus: 'from the 1st of November till the month of May, everything resumes new life; the suspended communications recommence; the roads are covered with waggons bringing from all quarters the produce of the interior; an immense number of carriages and single-horse chaises roll rapidly along – in short the commercial activity renders Charleston as lively as it is dull and melancholy in the summer'.

William was reassured by the change in the weather and went on to describe the refreshing Carolina climate in early winter – a less contentious subject than his expenses:

The climate answers to the description given of it with regard to the pure clear air at this season – we have an unclouded sky day and night for days nay weeks together, but if the Wind is anything northerly the mornings are very cold and air very thin, but towards noon it is as hot on the sunny side of the street as the hottest day in England and when it is southerly it is generally hot as July or August in England and such strong dews that the streets look in a morning as after heavy rain –

It will appear strange at first when I tell you that the rich planters are now returning to the country for the winter, it being the custom for them to flock here abt the 1st of Novr or till there has been a black frost or at least a keen northerly wind which destroys the noxious vapours which have arisen from the uncultivated swamps as also the Rice Swamps – It is found by experience that the Town and particularly the center of it is the most healthy during this season which I suppose is caused by the Fires correcting the air of its impurities – But in the interior where there are no swamps the air is always pure and salubrious –

William found himself despairing of doing any business in expensive Charleston, and was tempted to try one of the other smaller cotton centres in South Carolina and Georgia. Like all progressive thinkers, the Whittakers had disapproved of the slave trade in theory. But now William had seen the effects of slavery at first hand, he was uneasy about the practice and felt that it was as dangerous as it was immoral:

Cotton is very high, 15 or 16 dollars which with freight will be 18 d to 19 d in England – more than an average value without any profit – from what information I have been able to obtain Augusta is the place and something may be done to advantage but labour is very high and all is done by Slaves – this is called a free country, but very unjustly – Slaves are here as in the West Indies and from what I can learn their treatment

93

Slaves picking cotton on a Southern plantation. The planter wears the kind of summer clothes adopted by Charleston men.

little if any better and no doubt the same consequences will be the result as are now taking place in the West Indies

All the talk was about the 1791 slave revolt on Saint Domingue (the French part of the island of Santo Domingo, now Haiti) which had brought an influx of fleeing French settlers to the mainland. Charleston found the refugees, both black and white, fascinating, and welcomed them heartily. Many of them were well-educated doctors, businessmen, dancing teachers, musicians, cooks and bakers. They all enriched the cultural life of the city and gave it a characteristic French atmosphere. Their bloodcurdling stories of the revolt, however, including destruction of plantations, murder and mayhem, sent a shiver through the Carolina plantation owners.

Sympathy with France was rapidly to cool, however, when the city heard reports of the excesses of the French revolutionaries. After war broke out between Britain and France in 1793 and throughout the Napoleonic period, Charlestonians, like all Americans, were at odds with both the warring superpowers, Britain and France. Americans were furious at the high-handedness with which both of them treated American shipping, denying their 'right to freedom of the seas'. The British sometimes even boarded American ships and impressed their seamen into war service.

William obviously viewed the turbulent Charleston scene with anxiety and disapproval:

> . . . there are many French here from the difft islands but chiefly from St Domingo – some few respectable but in general Idle Vagabonds they have been brought up in Idleness and have neither Exertion nor Ability to get an honest livelihood and the most enterprizing are engaged in Privateering, which when at an end will have no honest means of gaining a living – there are also a vast number of French Mulattoes and Negroes who are ready for any mischief and since I have been here there have been 3 or 4 different attempts to set the Town on Fire, and once they so far succeeded that 3 houses were on fire but the alarm so soon given that they were extinguished before they got any head on, and as most of the Houses are of Wood only, the conflagration woud have been terrible – a person on looking out of his window observed a Mulatto with a light in his hand setting Fire to a wooden building opposite – where he got a Musket loaded with Buck Shot and Fired at him whereupon he fell but before the Gentleman coud get out he had got away –

Fire was a frequent and terrifying hazard in the wooden houses of Charleston, even when arson was not involved. It was said that citizens only felt safe when they lived within

sight and sound of St Michaels Church because a lookout
rang its bells as a fire alarm.

As William conversed with his fellow lodgers and new
acquaintances, he discovered that cotton buying was not the
only possibility for trade. There was another, more tempting
way to make money:

> In consequence of some conversation with Mr.
> Hussey of this house I have been almost tempted to take
> a trip into the West Indies – to Cape Francais in the
> island of St Domingo which you know is in the
> possession of the French with all inhabitants both
> Blacks and Mulattoes free – He went there about 6 mths
> ago with a cargo of Provisions at a time they were
> starving and dying in the streets – he remaind there
> about 3 mos. and has since been here making
> arrangements to go and settle there and open a store –
> he has a partner of the name of Brown, an Englishman,
> a young man who has been about 3 years in this country
> and lived at Wilmington in N Cara. where Mr H has
> resided some time since he returnd from the West Indies
> sick – Mr H has been above 13 years in the West Indies
> and has been at almost every Island –

The persuasive and knowledgeable Mr Hussey was particularly interested to know how much capital William had
available:

> In making enquiries of him about the Cotton trade
> here and likewise St. Domingo – he mentioned to me
> what he thought woud be attended by much greater
> advantage viz to embrace the present favourable
> opportunity of trading with the French part of St.
> Domingo – but remarked that the mode must be guided
> in a great measure by the extent of Capital. I told him
> I was aware of that and that at present £5 to £600 was
> as much as I coud command – He then proposed that
> as he had engaged part of a schooner to follow him with

more Goods in abt 10 days (he has now loaded a
schooner and sails in a day or too) he woud permit
anything of mine to be entered in his name for otherwise
the owner woud not take them, and it shoud be
understood by the Captain that I was going out as
Supercargo to him and had the charge of all his goods
to prevent anything unpleasant on account of my being
English – he likewise introduced me to the House of
Pippin [sic] and Co, most respected merchants, who
agreed to supply me with any Articles they had or woud
otherwise procure them on the best terms, for my drafts
endorsed by Mr Wallace, and charge me on the same
terms they had done Mr H, which I find upon enquiry
is about 5 to 10 per cent lower than the general Market
– He (Mr H) pointed out to me the Articles most current
and which I should have no difficulty in selling
immediately for cash and returning with the Value in
Coffee in which he assured me there woud be no doubt
of my making a handsome Profit – Mr. Pippin likewise
woud Insure the amount in his own Name against all
Risques whatever –

Joseph Peppin & Co were well-established merchants at
Gaillards Wharf in Charleston, and no doubt happy to supply
the goods for anyone innocent enough or rash enough to
hazard his capital at sea. Possibly Mr Hussey would receive
a commission for introducing a customer.

To William, eager for action, and swayed by the eloquence
of the helpful Mr Hussey, the idea of such a coup was
attractive. And yet he hesitated, writing down the different
courses of action in his letter and debating them as though
he were talking to his wife. She would receive his
deliberations weeks later, and feel frantic at her inability to
help him make up his mind what to do:

　. . . the whole of the business appeard to me so
eligible and so similar to what Mr Humble first proposed
when I talked of going to the West Indies – that I almost

concluded upon it, only made a reserve on account of not having received any letters from Europe – then again if I do not receive any soon I shall have been losing so much time, as I might compleat this plan in abt 2 mos. – and in all probability add about £200 to my Capital instead of consuming the Principal – and yet I wish to abide in great measure by what Mr Humble wants, and it is that only which prevents me –

Another factor made the idea of trading voyages uncertain, as William learned from an acquaintance, a British naval officer:

> There is a Lieutenant of an English frigate now here who was put on board a small schooner taken near the island of St Domingo, which was soon after retaken by a privateer and brought in here for four days past and since exchanged and at liberty to return for Jamaica where he is going in a few days –

Everyone had a story about the privateers which were such a menace to commercial houses. A privateer was a privately-owned vessel carrying a 'Letter of Marque' or commission from a sovereign state empowering her to seize declared enemies of that state on the high seas. Such seizures or prizes became the property of the captor.

Privateers were employed by both the British and French governments, and were a constant source of anxiety to merchants, captains and crews. They were a cheap weapon of war for governments, but for the owners, fitting out a privateer with arms and provisions for all-out commerce raiding was a heavy investment. Their risks and rewards were greater than normal cargo-carrying and the privateersmen they employed had to be bold and ready for a fight.

Most trading vessels carried double or triple sets of papers and sailed under as many flags as the privateer as she worked herself into hailing distance. French-commissioned privateers sailing from Charleston were tolerated long after northern ports had turned them away, though their swaggering crews of 'idle Vagabonds' eventually became as unpopular as the British.

William had also eagerly listened to the lieutenant's account of the war in the West Indies. English troops were steadily forcing forward in Saint Domingue, in the second year of a campaign to wrest the island from the French:

> I dined in his company yesterday and had an opportunity of making many enquiries abt the state of the English there as he only left it abt 2 mos ago – he says they have been much more healthy this year than last – that they are in possession of Port au Prince and another port the name I forgot commanding along the coast abt 50 miles and a considerable district interior likewise St Martin which commands a district abt as large – I asked him if he thought the British woud ever be able to reduce the whole island – he said he did not

A British naval party landing at Port Royal, Martinique, during the war in the West Indies, 1790s.

think so on account of the great number of the Inhabitants and the nature of the country . . .

In the previous year, 1794, the British expedition to Santo Domingo had been reduced to 1,600 men from 9,000, owing the ravages of yellow fever. In two years of war in the West Indies, 40,000 British soldiers were permanently stricken or died from disease. William ended his letter with a heartfelt plea to Sarah, his only link with home:

Now my dear Sarah I must make a conclusion and say something to Mr. Humble upon the subjects of business I have mentioned to you. Do my dear Wife let me hear from you often for you are my only correspondent and it is only by your means that I can hear of any part of our Family about whom I have many anxious moments as well as my dear Sarah and our dear little ones – Adieu

leaving this place at the most sickly season

Voyages to the West Indies, 1796

There is a gap of over a year between William's first long letter from Charleston and his next, in January 1797. Whether he ever made the voyage to Saint Domingue with Mr Hussey is not recorded, but he persevered with the idea of sea trading as a more attractive alternative to the cotton market. During 1796 he twice 'accepted an invitation' to sail to Jamaica, returning via Havana. These two voyages, his most spectacular and lamentably unsuccessful exploits, were recorded at some length. He described the difficulties of carrying on business in wartime with a letter of such frankness that Sarah's heart must have sunk as she read its ten closely-written pages.

It was abundantly clear that his real reason for the sea voyages was to escape the mortal terrors of the Charleston summer epidemics. It was not yet realised that yellow fever and malaria were carried by the mosquitoes which bred unchecked in the swampy interior.

Of all the fevers, the most feared was 'the black vomit' (yellow fever), a vile disease which started with chills and pains, was followed by the vomiting of black blood and finally a fatal haemorrhage. The most lethal outbreaks occurred in 1795, 1798 and 1799. Negroes on the plantations were relatively immune, and newly-arrived Europeans the most vulnerable, as they had no defences. The disease was known as 'Stranger's Fever'.

Doctors tried everything to effect a cure, from bleeding and cold water to calomel and violent purges. The most popular

101

treatments were sniffing rags dipped in vinegar, smelling camphor or tarred rope, smoking cigars or chewing garlic. Bark, wine, brandy and aromatics, plasters and mercury, tartar emetic and tamarind water were also tried as remedies. Some people whitewashed their houses, some burned gunpowder, some fired muskets from their windows.

Eventually it was realised that the infection came from the West Indies, and incoming ships were quarantined. It was also noticed that the cold weather usually ended the epidemics.

William Whittaker had feared for his life as the summer of 1796 approached, and though in his letter of January 1797 he tried to sound level-headed, the misery of the previous summer comes through plainly:

> Charleston has been uncommonly sickly and carried off a number of strangers – Spice taken in considerable quantities am informed since my return here is found to be a certain cure – those Europeans that have been here a few years and live well seem to stand it very well – the sickness began early in July and many died before I left, the 24th, and caused a great deal of alarm –
>
> In my former letters I mentioned my plans for making my first trip to Jamaica to pass the time when I coud see no prospect of doing anything to advantage here – my second trip was partly from the same motive, further induced from the prospect there was of profit, and also of leaving this place at the most sickly season . . .

Apart from the terror of mortal illness, the summer climate in Charleston was unbearably sultry. William must have soon abandoned his good Yorkshire clothes in the suffocating heat and thankfully adopted the Charleston gentleman's style of dress. All that could be worn with comfort was a light gingham short 'coatee', a linen waistcoat and white pantaloons, with a straw hat. The ladies wore the lightest of muslins.

Artist's impression of the exchange and harbour,
Charleston, in the 1790s.

In the heat of summer, people had to sleep under 'gauze pavilions' because of the mosquitoes. Charleston bedrooms in summer had all the drapes removed and beds were taken out into the middle of the room. The 'piazza' or verandah on the first floor of the larger houses always faced the south-west to shade the house from the sun and to catch every faint breeze from the sea.

One perspired at every pore even when sitting still, and mosquito bites were a continual torment. Sarah sent medical books and tried to find a good 'tropical application' to take away the inflammation, but the only real remedy was escape from the city.

William's letter on his return to Charleston from his sea voyages contained a very detailed account of business prices and conditions, which seems unusual in a letter to his wife. However, he knew her to be shrewd and intelligent, brought up in a family of businessmen, and that she would make a point of communicating every word to Mr Humble.

The Liverpool firm still paid scant attention to its

103

struggling agent. Perhaps resenting the imposition on their business of someone they thought ineffectual, the Liverpool office seemed to treat William with total indifference. Unfortunately, the unsuccessful trading trips he described so carefully and frankly were made using Mr Humble's money:

> With regard to profit we have been disappointed, owing to a combination of untoward and inexplicable circumstances – When we left Jamaica, Amn. [American] produce bore a high price, but soon after our return, accounts were received of the Arrival of Rice from India, and the consequent depreciation, which has had the effect to lower it here in a few days from 30/-to 25/- and even to 18/6, at which we bought some, and in a few days the remainder at 15/- Corn and peas, also Meal we had laid in, but they were little affected in proportion –

William's account of his blundering in the West Indian islands was painfully detailed. He seemed to confuse action, any action, with a well thought-out commercial plan. In 1796, however, even the most carefully thought-out business plan was likely to be upset. Not only did the high seas represent uncertainty, anxiety and peril from 'sea attaque and capture', but the politicans added their own brand of confusion.

As William explains, consternation among the Charleston merchants was extreme when William Pitt, Britain's wartime prime minister, unexpectedly brought a quantity of 'India rice' on to the market. This public relations exercise was designed to show the French that England would not starve in spite of French attacks on her shipping and American embargoes. It was conceded that the stroke was masterly, but in the New World many hearts sank along with their prices.

William wrote on with his catalogue of the summer's disasters:

> Instead of sailing the first week in July, it was the

25th, and afterwards a passage of 28 days gave many other vessels the chance of getting there first – and the high prices, as well as the bad treatment they experienced in French ports induced great numbers to flock to Jamaica, and in consequence all American produce has fallen by half and sometimes two thirds – Pork and Flour, which had fetched 22 to 24$ (this sign means dollars) was selling at 5 to 7$ – if we had given the top price of 28/- or 30/- for Rice we should have lost amazingly, but fortunately the articles we had held up better than many others, and though the nominal bore some profit, or saving, the commissions, freight, insurance etc. will take from my small capital a few hundred dollars –

I cannot however charge myself with any blame or neglect in this business – circumstances which were not foreseen were the cause of this unexpected depreciation, which gave a shock to the whole continent from which it has yet by no means recovered – This was brought about by Mr. Pitt's bringing a quantity of India Rice unexpectedly into the market, and at the same time a manoeuvre in stopping discounts preventing all specu-lation on provisions. It was considered by many here a masterpiece, and opened the eyes of many people who thought that to embargo Rice here would be to starve England –

Depressed by their bad luck and mistiming in Jamaica, and furious at the delays which compounded their misfor-tune, William and his companion, a Mr Harvie, sailed on to Cuba. Surely here their luck would turn. Alas, success continued to elude them, and to make matters worse, as soon as they had sailed, Jamaica prices rose tantalisingly again:

From Jamaica we proceeded to the Havana, with the intention of purchasing a cargo of molasses, but it was not the right season, and there was none at Market – we therefore bought Sugar, and if my companion Mr Harvie had at all extended himself, we might have got away before the Embargo was laid on, and as all our purchases were made we could take no advantage of a considerable fall which took place on War being declared [Spain and the Spanish colonies, including Cuba, joined France as an ally in October 1796] what we gave 8$ for sold at 6½$, so that we were out of luck at both places – for immediately after our leaving Kingston, provisions rose again and have continued very high, and another vessel from this place that was there and situated as we were, since has been another trip and made a great voyage – but the French take all the Amrn. vessels bound to British ports, and Insurance is treble the usual price –

Molasses were just coming in, and I bought a cask on leaving the Havana for 33$, which sold here for 67$, 3 of which goes for duty, so you see we should have had a fine harvest if we could have loaded with it, and it has since fallen in a proportion of 10 to 8 – A very

Havana on the island of Cuba, 1807.

106

advantageous trade might be carried on betwixt this and Jamaica, but the times are too precarious at present –

'The Havana', the capital city of the Spanish island of Cuba, was a most important trading port, only a fortnight's sail away from Charleston. The wealth of Spanish inhabitants was said to be 'enormous, almost incredible' explained Charles Cotton, another Englishman and a teacher at Charleston College, urging his brother, a naval surgeon, to come and try his hand at the 'Havannah' trade. Beside its foreign trade, he explained, Havana was 'the rendezvous of the Spanish Register or money ships, from Vera Cruz and Carthagena to old Spain'.

It seems clear that the idea of making one's fortune by taking a ship to Cuba, Santo Domingo, Jamaica or the Spanish Main was a much discussed and popular subject among Charleston traders. Charles Cotton was just as ingenuously enthusiastic over prospects in his own letters to England: 'In this country there are so many ways of turning money to a good account – Ten per cent is frequently made in the way of interest; almost everyone here possessed of any capital speculates in landed property, the produce of the country, or merchandise . . . Merchants here drive a very gainful clandestine trade to the Spanish Main, La Vera Cruz, New Orleans & c. in swift-sailing schooner vessels, which tho' attended with the risk of capture by British and French cruisers, is very successfully carried on, at an enormous profit of from 150 pounds to 200 and 300 per cent.'

The air was thick with stories, excitedly spread, of magnificent coups and brilliant round trips.

'I can assure you from the lips of a young man who has just returned from the Cruize', wrote Charles Cotton, 'that a brig, loaded by our Merchants, took a freight of dry goods, (such as muslins &c.) to Vera Cruz in Mexico valued at 20,000 dollars, received for the cargo in hard money without any difficulty 80,000 Dollars, laid out a great part in Sugars of the same place which return a profit here of cent p. cent

[100%], loaded all their guns to the muzzle with the remainder of the Dollars, to elude seizure, the Spaniards constantly prohibiting the export of gold and silver, and have safely returned here to the great joy of the owners and a most valuable cargo of Sugars and Dollars. It is a fact that the treasures destined for old Spain, which, for fear of being captured by the British ships are detained at Vera Cruz, are so immense, that the dollars may be seen piled up in prodigious heaps to the amount of many millions sterling. The Havannah is perfectly glutted with American produce and dry goods. Even flour which commonly brings 20 dollars a barrel sells for no more than six or seven, tho' here it is eight or nine dollars. Coffee is extremely high and brings great profit, here and in Europe. Trade on the whole is very brisk.'

Unfortunately, by the time it was rumoured in the coffee houses and taverns that everyone was making a fortune, the opportunity had really gone. It was speculative madness which was rife. After his return to Charleston, however, William at least had first-hand information on the state of trade with the Cuban capital, which was 'precarious' now that Spain had entered the war. He had found that:

> Trade to the Havana is too circumscribed, as they don't allow any foreign vessels to enter unless they have Negroes and Ballast, but it is on the way home from Jamaica. Indeed all trade to the West Indies is at present precarious, and it is generally expected that an Embargo will be laid on in all the United States.

William's first hurried note, recording his return to Charleston in January 1797, described making good his escape from Cuba:

> . . . having just heard that a vessel is ready to sail and has just dropt down to the Bar, I will not omit writing a few lines to say I am returnd safe to Charleston – We embraced the first fair wind after the Embargo was taken off to leave the Havana and had the good fortune

to arrive here in 9 days without meeting any Enemies or any accidents.

The 'Embargo' which had delayed William's return to Charleston, and is so frequently mentioned in his account of his 1796 voyages, was a favourite economic weapon of war, used in this instance by Cuba. An embargo denied the use of ports to foreign ships, for periods varying from a few weeks to months at a time. A series of embargoes was the only device open to the American Congress which really hurt the two great powers, Britain and France. Embargoes were designed to make life even more difficult for those engaged in trade.

The Americans felt continuing bitterness towards both the French and British naval forces and privateers. American ships, officially neutral, were subjected by both powers to the indignity of 'stop and search'. Charles Cotton had actually felt so furious on behalf of his American friends that he wrote home: 'We are incensed to see the British flag violate so frequently its good faith to this country. The papers are frequently announcing fresh insults on the American flag by British frigates and privateers, both of whom are little better than pirates in the West Indies, and in these seas. So much for British protection . . .'

William's long letter of February 1797, describing his second voyage, began with a glimpse of the appalling difficulties of communication. On his return he had found that mail awaiting him dated only from the previous August:

> After an absence of near 6 mos. I again sit down in my quarters to chat a la distance with my ever dear Sarah – I need not inform you that I grew very anxious to hear from you and that I was made very happy by so many pleasing accounts of yourself, the Dear Children and the Knutsfordians – your accounts of the last as well as their own by Mary and Frances [William's sisters] have given me great comfort indeed –
> There have been two arrivals here from London which

bring papers and letters up to the third week in
November but none for me since August – the last from
Liverpool dated Augst 23rd – Some paint that Mr
Humble's house was sending me by way of trial was lost,
the vessel being wrecked on the coast of Georgia, but
it would not have answered had it come safe, there being
only one person here who prepares it – he fixes his own
price – it was by this vessel that you sent the Books,
Cravats, Shirts etc. – of course they were lost – don't
trouble yourself to send the books, as Chisholm is to be
sold here and most likely the others will be available –

William also related the story of another typical privateer-
ing attack successfully countered by bold seamen:

The ship Derby of this place from London arrived 2
Days ago, after having been taken by the French, and
afterwards retaken by the Captain, 2 Mates and 4
Hands, who watched their opportunity and rose upon
the 12 men put aboard by the French privateer – They
put the Frenchmen adrift in the Longboat within sight
of Hispaniola [Santo Domingo], and proceeded in safety
to their port.

Having reduced his capital through injudicious trading
trips by sea, William now had no option but to turn back to
cotton, this time not to buying and selling, but to the industry
itself.

The invention of the cotton gin or 'engine' by Eli Whitney,
a simple but brilliant device, had given the American cotton
industry a tremendous fillip since 1793. The cotton gin was
so quick and effective at cleaning the seeds and dirt from the
cotton that the Americans gained a tremendous advantage
over their competitors in India, South America and the West
Indies, who could not find a satisfactory cleaning method.
Perhaps there was a fortune to be made in the processing side
of the raw cotton industry?

Sadly, there had been a major fire in Savannah – a type

The first cotton gin, invented by Eli Whitney in 1793.

of recurring disaster just as much feared by the people of Charleston:

Cotton I find is low and sale in England, and if the War continues I shoud think likely to continue so – on my return here I partly concluded with myself to go to Savannah and begin the Cotton Cleaning unless there was a prospect of peace soon, but my capital being reduced instead of increased (as I had hoped) by losses and the expences of living, is a great obstacle, and the circumstances of so great a part of the Town being burned will make it difficult and expensive to establish a place – I mentioned in my last letter that of 500 abt 340 houses were destroyed in Savannah by fire during my last absence – If an Embargo takes place, I will attempt it upon a plan proportionate to my means, as Cotton will be very low, and in short everything the produce of this country –

111

The Charleston merchants gambled heavily on cotton. The business climate was frantic, and William probably recognised an unpleasant if familiar atmosphere:

> You say Mr Humble was glad I had not purchased – so am I, when I saw how business was carrying on here – the merchants are all amazing speculators, and in short it is more like a regular System of Gambling than mercantile proceedings. They are so much embarrassed in consequence of having so far overtraded themselves last year to such great loss, and their purchases at such high prices, for notes only, which have scarce any been discharged but renewed by lending and borrowing, that it is hard to say who of any of them are safe – if they were independent of each other, one half woud have fallen to the ground already, and now it is doubtful if two thirds in a string do not fall together, as the most adventurous are pulling the more prudent as deep into the mud as themselves.

William should certainly have been aware of the many pitfalls of speculation after his previous experiences in Manchester. But he had already been drawn, by the persuasive talk of Mr Hussey, Mr Harvie and even Messrs Peppin & Co the wholesale merchants, into risking his capital at sea and losing most of it. Gambling was as prevalent a disease as the fever – but it seemed better than idleness. He went on:

> If you hear of an Embargo or there shoud not be arrivals from here you must not be surprized as it may be laid on any day now – In my letter to Mr Humble's Ho. I have not communicated so fully as to you, for I do not know how far they may be acquainted with circumstances – I never receive any letters direct from Mr H. – only from the House – So far I have written to you by the ship Eliza, Captain Macneal for London this 25th Feby, of which the above is merely a copy as there

is a risk of vessels bound for England being carried into
France –

At the end of this long letter, William finally turned to
more domestic matters:

> You direct me to send you some Bulbs, but I can
> assure you I have not seen anything of the kind in this
> country – there are few gardens about Town and merely
> for Culinary purposes, and those in the country attend
> very little ornamental, but as I shall be here this coming
> spring, I shall have an opportunity of seeing more than
> I have done –

Sarah, whose letters always show a keen love of gardens,
had probably heard that Charleston was noted for the
luxuriance of its plants and flowers. Since the eighteenth
century, its gardens and plantations have been famous –
nowadays for their magnificent camellias, magnolias,
azaleas, wisteria and jasmine, as well as their moss-draped
live oaks and palm trees.

William apparently saw nothing of this – perhaps he
walked through the city unseeingly, his head full of money
problems. No doubt, too, he was excluded from the estates
and gardens of the rich by his lack of success and
connections.

But at least William could report that he had some cheerful
company in his anxious and lonely hours – not, however, with
Charleston friends:

> I forgot to mention that I have got a parrot for Sarah,
> and one for Wm., or whoever you think proper if you
> think one will be enough – they are both at it now
> Whistleing, Singing, Talking, Trumpeting and Hollow-
> ing – I got them young at the Havana so that they only
> speak English – I never enter my room but I am saluted
> with How do you do? How do you do, my dear? – Never
> mind – What's all this about then? – Polly, Polly, Polly,

113

Pretty Poll – and they are attempting several tunes – they are very fine Birds, natives of Vera Cruz on the Main – green with much yellow on the head – Feby. 22nd – as a vessel is going for Liverpool and the letter bag is going on board in half an hour, I must conclude my dear Sarah, Yrs ever, most truly,

W. Whittaker.

hope deferrd wch maketh the heart sick

Years of Stress, 1799-1804

As the century drew to a close, William and Sarah remained parted by the Atlantic Ocean and both showed increasing signs of stress. Mr Tipping remained obdurate in refusing to sign William's certificate of discharge from bankruptcy. The Whittakers could not understand this continued harshness, and Sarah decided on an appeal to Mrs Tipping, woman to woman. She wrote on the 2nd April 1799, lengthily, with elaborate dignity:

Madam,

Encouraged by the consciousness of never having intentionally injured or offended, I take the liberty of addressing you upon a subject a Wife and Mother must feelingly comprehend – Tis nearly 4 years (29 April 1795) since Mr Whittaker quitted England – during this interval I have been encouraged from time to time to hope that a period to our separation woud arrive – unwilling to expose my Children to the various perils of banishment I have continued to look forward, but time seems to bring nothing but that hope deferrd wch maketh the heart sick...Considering it within the power of Mr Tipping to restore a Father to my children or involve us all in a common exile, Tis your Active Sympathy, dear Madam, wch I earnestly entreat.

There was no answer.

115

William wrote from Charleston in March 1799 after returning from another stay in Cuba:

> I have once more the pleasure of addressing my dear Sarah from a land of liberty, whence I can communicate more freely than for a long time past –

There is a flavour of paranoia about this letter, suffused as it is with the fear of being spied on by his creditors or even thrown into gaol in America. His whereabouts may have been discovered and threats may have followed him to Charleston, or else the frightening stories of other debtors on the run were serving to unhinge him. Being an Englishman was itself a disadvantage among the patriotic Americans and the Spanish:

> I forget the date of your last, having from prudential motives destroyed every letter, paper and even memo that might cause suspicion to the jealous, arbitrary people amongst whom I have lately sojourned – in consequence of having seen many in similar situations with myself being taken up and thrown into a loathsome prison without being allowed the least communication or knowledge of an offence untill they have ransacked and overhauled their papers – and all this on mere suspicion or on the information of some villain who from motives of Jealousy and a consciousness of their own inferiority cannot endure strangers.
>
> I however was fortunate not to be troubled in the very least, although I know several informations were given to the Govr.

William's fears also included the possibility of an imminent involvement in a hostile raid on Havana – presumably by British naval forces:

> As there was an alarm that the place was going to be attackd and orders came out to act in all cases as though

the enemy was in sight, I thought it a good time to come
here to settle some business –

He intended to return to Cuba within a fortnight, he
explained, trying to convey the impression that his with-
drawal had been planned and not a headlong flight:

> I shall endeavour to do something more beneficial to
> myself in the commercial line, having the assurance of
> many friends both here and to the Northward, that I
> shall have a preference, there being a general disgust
> of the method in which it has been carried out by the
> Establishd houses – and though I have not betterd my
> circumstances much I have the satisfaction of having
> gaind the good opinion of many who traded to the
> Havana –

In fact, it was not only spies, informers and possible
hostilities he wanted to flee, but also business unpleasant-
ness with a former associate: 'my leaving at this time also
enabled me to leave Mr F [Fraser] upon a more friendly
footing than I coud otherwise have done –'

He also reiterated his determination to make 'every
restitution to those who have been injured' in England, and
pointed out that:

> it is their duty equally to assist me with all their power
> to enable me to do it. So far as that it is withheld I do
> and shall consider myself exonerated from obligation,
> and will always be on my guard to resist attempts made
> by individuals to force partial advantage – I consider
> myself equally under obligation to all –

William's fear of spies and informers made him urge Sarah
to be on her guard at all times:

> In your letters continue to express yourself in the most
> guarded manner as it has become more necessary than
> ever, and if you mention names, let it be only in initials,

117

or where that may not be sufficient make use of the following letters as J. Buck J Code –instead of figures I shall make use of the following letters g u s t a m w o r h n (1 2 3 4 5 6 7 8 9 0), as I may in future wish to communicate to you what I would wish only yourself to know – I shall send a duplicate of this as I am apprehensive several of mine may have miscarried lately, from the custom Captains of Vessels have of destroying letters in the appearance of an armd vessel whether friend or foe – Avoid all Politicks likewise and let me hear from you frequently –

I was surprized to find your packet off brig Margaret on my arrival here – it had lain at the Post office since I left this, and had been opened – there was an open letter from Mary and William's letter and drawing but none from yourself – two Books on the fever and some pamphlets and a Shirt and a cravat – and in one of the books some beautiful affecting lines by your own pen, but by whom they may have been perused I cannot tell – The Books I have not had time to read but shall on my return – the Weather has been very cool since I came here and I have found much benefit from it as from the Voyage – Remember me most affly and Kiss our Little Folks –

William's efforts to conceal his movements made him adopt an alias, that of 'William Wade', and prudence also led him to apply for an American passport, which has survived with his papers. Concealing his nationality as well as his name could not only help him to evade the importunings of his creditors, but would also be helpful in business.

On a United States letterhead with eagle and the motto *E Pluribus Unum*, the passport is headed 'Consulate of Havana. Mr Geo. C. Morton, V-Consul of the United States of America for the City of Havana &c':

I do hereby certify that on the day and date thereof

118

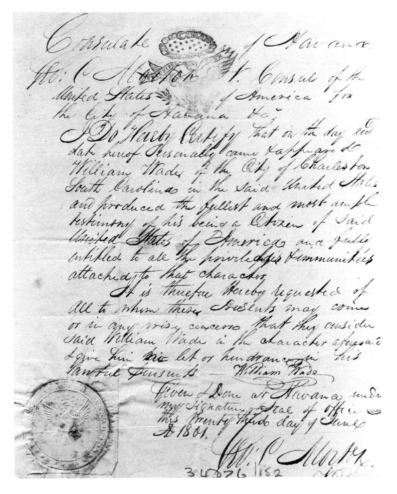

The American passport of William Whittaker, using the
false name William Wade, 1801.

personally came and appeared William Wade of the City
of Charleston South Carolina in the said United States
and produced the fullest and most ample testimony of
his being a citizen of the said United States of America
and fully entitled to all the privileges and immunities
attached to that character.

119

It is therefore Hereby requested of all to whom these present may come or in any wise concern, that they consider said William Wade in the character aforesaid and give him no let or hindrance in his lawful pursuits
Signed William Wade.

The passport was 'given and done at Havana under the signature and Seal of the Consulate of Havana on the twenty-third of June AD 1801'.

It is not clear why William suffered bad relations with Mr Fraser in Cuba, from whom he was glad to part order to avoid too many recriminations, but he acquired and kept a copy of an enigmatic letter sent by another businessman, Thomas Hill, on the 17th February 1801 after enquiries from a firm in England. Mr Hill apparently regarded Mr Fraser as shockingly unprincipled:

> Gentn.,
> Your esteemd favor dated 12st ult reached me two days past and I hasten a reply to the same that you may give as early advice to your correspondent in England as possible –
> You could not (although it has occurred by chance) have made application to a person more proper than myself – the business is so interwoven with a certain Character, an intimate of Mr Reid's, who is absconded himself from hence in a very unhandsome manner, as to prevent an other than a personal communication proper – I have therefore declined giving particulars in a letter but have made up my mind to pay you a visit. I shall probably embark a few days from hence.

At least part of Charles Fraser's iniquities appear to have been connected with a fraudulent insurance claim on the loss of the ship *General Goddard*, and with debts he owed to Mr Hill – and probably also to William:

> the intimate friend of Mr Reid's is no less a personage than Mr Charles Fraser, the merchant at whose instance

120

I addressed your respectable house on the subject of the Genl Goddard. He has left heavy sums unpaid and to myself a few thousand Dollars – I shall endeavour to gain every additional information on the business in point and if I can by such Testimony as will prevent a fraud of such magnitude taking place, I shall not be the loser –

The letter hints that it would all be much simpler were there any funds available to pay for information – which the 'respectable house' had obviously refused. The difficulties were compounded by the fact that the absconding Fraser owed money to Spanish businessmen too:

Was I authorized I coud obtain it by giving a gratuity to a certain person on whom entirely depends the chief testimony to invalidate the Insurance – the difficulty of getting Depositions from Spaniards at any time is great but more particularly, clearly, at this juncture – Where there is an appearance of property, though in the name of another, yet belongs to (or partly so) to a Man absconded largely in Debt to the Spaniards makes it delicate and difficult. I will only add that there never was a more unjust transaction.

For every brilliantly successful eighteenth century entrepreneur who came back to England with a fortune, founding myths of the great opportunities available for all, there must have been a hundred who floundered like William. His business affairs never ran smoothly, he was frequently cheated and in fact he seemed to lurch from crisis to crisis.

He was probably too gentle, too gullible and perhaps too ineffectual to succeed in the free-for-all, unscrupulous and often desperate trading atmosphere of the New World. He must have been often acutely despondent, whether he blamed others for his failures or recognised his own weaknesses and shortcomings.

Although Sarah never lost her loyal confidence in his

121

integrity, it is likely that he sailed too close to the wind in increasing despair at his inability to make any financial headway.

In 1803, William found himself again in difficulties – as the defendant in a lawsuit brought by his Spanish former partner in Havana, Mr Motta, who was probably trying to recover his investment in their trading trips. Perhaps the unwary Mr Motta had not appreciated that the gentlemanly 'Mr William Wade', the 'American' merchant from Charleston, was an undischarged bankrupt, still terrified of his English creditors nine years after his bankruptcy. But William defended himself with his customary rectitude.

When he returned to England in 1804, William brought with him this copy of the instructions he had left with Mr Madan, who was to represent him in the quarrel with Motta. The statement of accounts gives an interesting insight into William's business activities.

His partnership with Mr Motta in Havana had expired, it seems, in a welter of recriminations. Money was still owing to William from three ventures with Mr Motta, including profit on the sale of slaves. The fact that William was trading in slaves seems sad evidence of moral decline in the face of expediency since his first days in the New World, when he expressed his indignation at their treatment in the United States.

Monies still owing in Charleston are listed, and William declares that he can't pay Mr Motta anything until he has discharged these debts. He also insists that when he left Motta he took not a penny from the concern. He ends his defence with a list of debts and powers of attorney against Mr Motta in Havana, which he thinks Mr Motta should pay:

That several items left blank remain to be brought into the account of which no accounts have been rendered to the Defendant, such as nett proceeds on Segars, half profit on Negroes with Sta. Maria, Interest in Schn [schooner] Picket, card.[carried] to Providence claimd and recd by Maines, Mackie & Co of Savana [*sic*]

That there remain several Debts, dues and unpaid sundries in Charleston, the attornies for whom are always referrd to the defendant [William Whittaker] for payment by Mr Motta. And until these Debts are discharged the Defendant coud not in justice to himself even if it were in his power pay anything to Mr. Motta.

The list included $1,700 owed to Joseph Peppin & Co, $1,800 to Patrick Gibson, $900 to I C Graesen, $1,200 to Mr Green and $400 to Miss Huxans – $6,000 in total.

William's statement continued:

On the Defendant separating from Mr Motta he had not taken a Dollar from the concern – the capital remaining entirely with Mr M [Motta].

There followed another list of debts and powers of attorney 'in Havana agst. I.P. de la M [Mr Motta]'.

Chauveteau for Peppin & Co was owed $1,700, and 'for his own Debt 600$'. Martin Madan was owed $500 as an agent, and $500 on his own account, and Poey & Co for Barker & Lord were owed $2,200. These debts amounted to $5,500.

William's return to England in 1804 was forced, when he discovered, no doubt to his consternation, that he was subpoenaed as a witness in a trial in London connected with the allegedly absconding and fraudulent Charles Fraser, and that he must use his own name in court.

He feared that the publicity of the trial and his arrival in England could be dangerous, but naturally husband and wife longed to see each other and at least his expenses were being met by the legal authorities. Sarah thought it would be a good opportunity to try once again to obtain his discharge, and she fervently hoped he would never have to return to the United States.

He dared not come to Yorkshire, but during the summer of 1804 stayed at Belvedere House in Bath, the home of his friends the Reverend Thomas and Mrs Broadhurst. Sarah visited him here for a loving reunion. Their happiness at seeing each other again after nearly ten years of parting was overwhelming. A curious little postscript to one of her letters – 'that which we feared in Bath did not come to pass' – may have been meant to reassure him that their meeting would not result in another child.

the most awful moment of my life

A Difficult Winter, 1804

William made several trips to see lawyers in London and resolved to stay over the winter in England, even if the trial to which he had been summoned was completed. Another fruitless attempt to gain his discharge from bankruptcy followed, and his brother Daniel in Liverpool sent a loyal letter full of indignant sympathy.

William's own nature must have been extraordinarily attractive, to judge by the unswerving family love and loyalty

The Court of Chancery, Lincolns Inn, 1807.

125

with which he was always surrounded. He must have smiled rather ruefully at his brother's fervour.

'Obdurate Hearts!', exclaimed Daniel with a flourish. 'How can such men who cannot forgive their Brother for the loss of a little paltry pelf in this world, ever with confidence address the Almighty to forgive them their sins? I abhor such Characters – I hear on your return Mrs W has made up her mind to accompany you, let me know if you are likely to take Shipping from hence – We shall be very happy to see you & of your bitter Enemies shall pray God may abate their Pride, assuage their Malice, and confound their Devices. Keep up your Spirits, I hope you will live to rise superior to them all –

I recd. your Segars wch proved very good Smoaking, accept my thanks for the Trouble in procuring them and be so good as to give Mr Humble's house an order on me and the money shall be paid to them.'

During that autumn Daniel wrote frequently, quizzing William about current conditions in the cotton states. First-hand knowledge was like money in the bank to the cotton broker, and indeed to all the businessmen of Liverpool and Manchester. Any returning commercial man found himself in great demand.

Daniel particularly wanted to hear news of the 'Hurricane in Georgia and Carolina' and wished to know 'your friends confidential and real state of damage and state of the Cotton Plantations and promise of what may be expected of the late crops'.

In December 1804, anxious to exchange information and business leads with William, he wrote:

The enclosed Letter was receiv'd yesterday it came by the Eliza from Savannah or Packet from Boston, both of which arrived, also the South Carolina and Prosperity from Philadalphia, and as the Wind is fair we expect many in daily from Amern Ports – recent Accts from Georgia and Carolina are said to bring worse Accts of destruction to the Cottonstock and Plantations than formerly —

He included a comprehensive list of cotton prices, included those for 'Bowd Georgias', Sea Islands, 'Barbads' (Barbados), 'Demera' (Demerara) and Berbice in Guiana, and Bahia and 'Pernambucco' in Brazil.

Cotton from the Sea Islands off the Carolina coast was the finest long-staple variety, and Georgia Bowd, a strong short-staple cotton in demand for serviceable cotton fabrics, was to become the South's biggest seller. The name 'Bowd' came from the practice of vibrating a bow in the cotton, which, rather inefficiently, sent the seeds flying out.

Daniel continued:

> You will assist me by any recommendations you can give for Consignments from respectable Houses to us of Amern or other Produce, also Ships as we are in a general line of Agency Commission and brokerage business, and have a knowledge of most Articles — anything coming through you here shall be happy in dividing the Commn with you.

Daniel's brisk business correspondence must have acted like a tonic for William, as the idle months made him very low in spirits, and deference to his American knowledge must have raised his self-esteem. Perhaps Daniel's letters had this kindly intention.

As the autumn advanced, Sarah decided that the role of quiet and patient wife did not suit her temper any longer. It seemed to her, frustrated beyond belief by the obduracy of their enemies, that the gentlemanly diffidence with which William had pursued his case for discharge was reaping no rewards at all.

'It is ten years since our ruined family quitted Manchester', she wrote histrionically in a summary of her story up to 1804 which she kept among her papers:

As Mr. Tipping had been a great sufferer it was not thought either prudent or delicate to be early in applying for a certificate. After my husband had quitted England, myself and children subsisted on a portion of my property secured to me by our marriage writings and wch exactly produced 100£ per annum – Our attempts at intervals of two or three years to secure our creditors' signatures to the discharge certificate had been unavailing. But if resentment shoud not have subsided in ten years it scarce ever woud –

What if she should now take a hand in the matter herself? She felt sure she could succeed where her husband had failed – she knew that she was persuasive, still an attractive woman, and with the personality to demonstrate her case in a dramatic fashion. Could Mr Tipping and his cohorts of legal advisers, the other creditors and their manifold heirs and successors, withstand a personal appeal from Sarah? She thought not.

She decided to go to Manchester and make a desperate effort to plead William's case in person, staying with friends who had promised to do everything they could to help her.

On Thursday the 29th November she arrived at the Bridgewater Arms at midnight to be met by her friend Mr Spear who, she related in a letter to William, 'conveyed me and my baggage to his home'. There she met Mr Halliwell, Mr Tipping's partner, who had also promised to befriend the Whittakers.

Mr Spear suggested it might be best to wait upon Mr Tipping at Ardwick, where the suppliant 'might have the benefit of Mrs T's influence'. Sarah, having not found the lady responsive to her earlier appeals, felt that she would have a better chance if she dealt only with the more susceptible sex.

It had been arranged that she would meet Mr Tipping's attorney, Mr Eccles, on Friday, in the somewhat naive hope of persuading him to use his influence on her behalf.

Sarah's friend Mrs Simpson had promised her assistance, and it was from Hart Hill, her elegant home in Salford, that the next day the two ladies set off for the attorney's rooms. Mrs Simpson was a formidable ally, as her late husband John had been a partner with Richard Arkwright's son in the first steam-powered mill in Salford and an influential figure among the cotton manufacturers.

It was not until Sunday that Sarah had recovered her composure enough to describe the events of that stressful Friday and Saturday in her letter to William in Bath. On Friday evening, she had to have frequent recourse to the smelling bottle, and kind Mrs Simpson was obliged to administer a glass of strong cordial to her swooning friend.

Mr Eccles seemed pleasant enough at the first interview, and told Sarah and Mrs Simpson that Mr Tipping's resentment was 'long got over'. He was only prevented from signing the certificate by an agreement with some of the other creditors. Were she to see Mr Tipping and obtain their names, he thought things could be easily arranged.

After this interview, the two ladies, with Mr Halliwell, got into their carriage and drove to Thomas Tipping's Cannon Street offices. Sarah wrote:

> Mrs Simpson and Mr Halliwell accompanied me to a very alarming interview at his Compting House – they entered first and were graciously received – but as soon as I appeard an expression of the utmost horror and rage animated his Countenance – he just said 'How could you serve me so, Mr Halliwell!' and rushed past me – I followed and seized his hand, and entreated to be heard but he burst from me with the energy of a Madman and I suppose did not stop until he reached Ardwick. His agitation and anger on seeing me were so extreme that I sank upon his steps in the bitterest anguish and despair.

Sarah's hopes were thus brutally dashed. She got into the

carriage again in a state of shock and they drove to the house of Mrs Hyde, the widow of one of the creditors:

> My friends persuaded me go on to see Mrs Hyde, the executor of Mr Hyde's estate, and scarce knowing what I did I drove there, but from that lady I gained just as I expected, nothing.

Sarah and Mrs Simpson drove back to Hart Hill, and in spite of its civilised comforts, Sarah spent a 'miserable night'.

The next morning, however, brought a surprise which revived her spirits – an unexpected visit from Mr Eccles, the lawyer. Her story continued:

> Guess the surprize and joy with wch I was seized when I found him charged with a most kind message from Mr Tipping expressing concern for his reception of me – seeing me so suddenly had deprived him of all command of himself – he regretted the pain he had caused me and had neither eaten nor slept himself since that moment. He had not intended to wound my feelings and his own had been deeply affected. Mr Eccles reported also that Mr Tipping agreed to sign the certificate and was to persuade Mrs Hyde to do the same.
>
> I am glad to tell you Ridgway's abode [another creditor] is discovered (the Grecian Coffee House, London), but Mr Eccles now thinks his presence will not be required – Hyde's signature is all we want – Mr Tipping allows Jones to sign wch will make up the number and then Mr T. himself will sign for the value – Adieu my dear William write to me immediately and mention what name will be used at the trial – I think if we don't succeed now our kind friend Mrs Simpson will feel the disappointment almost as acutely as myself.

Bankrupts could only obtain their discharge, according to the rules of the time, if four-fifths of the creditors signed the certificate. Those to whom was owed not less than four-fifths

of the value must also sign, and no creditor owed less than
£20 could make up the number in value. This tortuous
provision had no time limit and caused the endless years of
punishment endured by bankrupts like William. Later laws
limited the time during which creditors could refuse to sign
the certificate of discharge from bankruptcy. Today a
bankruptcy will normally be wound up within three years.

On Saturday evening, restored to composure, and even
relishing the task, Sarah had penned an apology to Mr
Tipping regretting her behaviour in her most elegant phrases.
It was essential to restore her dignity after the unladylike
commotion she had caused. She included this copy of it in
her letter to William:

Hart Hill, Saturday night Nov. 1804

Sir,

With every sentiment of Respect and Gratitude I
cannot forbear the expression of them for the very kind
messages you enabled Mr Eccles to convey to me – the
consideration of my Duties as a Wife and Mother (for
on you depend all my future comforts and the temporal
perhaps Eternal Welfare of my children) gave me
resolution and support in what I felt to be *the most awful
moment of my life* . . . little suspecting that any heart
but my own woud suffer by the exertion, my Surprize
and grief were extreme to witness the Emotion my
presence had excited in a face whch I had been used to
behold and revere as the Index of a Benevolent Mind,
but believe me Sir my feelings even at that Dreadful
Moment were not confined to my own Sufferings & I
deeply regret that I took a Step so painful to Both

After I left Cannon Street Despair took complete
possession of me, and when the next morning Mr Eccles
told me that Mr Tipping had not only expressed regret
for my Suffering but had actually released Mrs Hyde
from her engagement, I coud scarcely believe the
evidence of my senses – and I find joy almost as difficult

to bear as Sorrow. Indeed the necessity whch once threatened me of forsaking either my Husband or my Children wd I think have overpowerd my Reason & I can never be sufficiently grateful to you for averting so dreadful an alternative – I hope, Sir, to hear from Mr Eccles on Thursday that you no longer suffer from the consequences of my intrusion, and that you and yours may long enjoy every domestic comfort whch worldly prosperity and approving hearts can bestow is the warmest prayer of your much obliged and sincerely grateful Sarah Whittaker.

Confident that her intervention had been successful, Sarah returned to Bradford, travelling with Michael Humble in his carriage. But she still had further depths of shame to plumb, and was horrified when Mr Humble, who appeared to be following the whole affair closely, broached 'with all possible delicacy' a new problem which Mr Greg, one of the executors of another deceased creditor, had asked him to raise with her:

> Wednesday afternoon Mr Greg started a new difficulty – a Disgust he had conceived toward me on account of my conduct on leaving the Farm [at Moss Side] – That it was well known we possessed a large quantity of fine Table Linen, not an article of which had been exposed to Sale – also a considerable quantity of Plate (among wch was a Silver Tea Urn) and Books I had conveyed away – You may judge how Mr Humble wd feel on such a charge from wch (being entirely ignorant of these matters) he could not exculpate me and scarce knew how to reveal to me . . .

The cold truth was now obvious. Although Sarah had discreetly addressed all her letters to 'Mr William Wade' in Bath and London, William's return to England was common knowledge and the forthcoming London trial the subject of gossip and rumour. Reasons were being found by his creditors for framing delays in the hope that the outcome of the trial would mean a settlement from the insurers for William, and thus more money for them. They also proposed to hound Sarah over the sale of her possessions.

Sarah wrote on the 6th December:

> It is very unlucky that the trial commences just at this time, and particularly if you are obliged to give your own name. What astonished and vexd me extremely was a conversation I had with Mrs Simpson yesterday in wch she told me it was generally known you were come to England upon a trial and for wch you were to receive your travelling expenses and 50£ a month − I was perfectly Thunderstruck with this intelligence and enquired from whom she receivd it − she says it is several months ago it was not mentioned as any secret.

She exhorted William to be punctilious in his behaviour and added some useful information gleaned from Francis Duffield:

> I think you must have misunderstood Mrs Tayler's attorney respecting the necessity of your appearance before the Lord Chancellor − Mr Duffield says that is not requisite − but you must make an affidavit before a Master in Chancery (with wch every county town is provided) that you have given up all your property − whether this alludes only to the property you had when you became a Bankrupt or extends to any property you may have become possessed of since − ought to be thoroughly understood. If the latter & you shoud have received any compliment from the Insurers you cannot make such an affidavit − & I wish your conduct to be such as were every article laid before the public wd not only justify you in your own conscience but in the opinion of the world and your creditors − some of whom woud be glad of a Handle to continue inexorable −

Sarah's letters were endlessly filled with discussion of the creditors, the executors and their delays, but she perhaps

133

grew weary of the subject herself as the weeks went on. Christmas brought some welcome relief at Townhill, when her young half-brother John Buck arrived for the holiday. There was distressing news of a friend who had fallen in battle a hero, in the Indian Mahratta Wars with Sir Arthur Wellesley:

> I practise Corelli and Purcells music along with J.B.'s violoncello – he is all spirits and good humour – I found Mrs. D but poorly but she is now better – I had a letter from Sarah White yesterday containing some particulars of poor Tom – His conduct was so distinguished that orders were issued by the Commander-in-Chief for erecting a Marble Tomb over his remains at Agra. He received the Fatal wound in endeavouring to Bring off Mr Grant – the situation he was in was extremely exposed – every artillery Man at a 6 pounder was either killd or wounded –

The Whittaker children were spending Christmas with William's sisters at Knutsford and Sarah reported:

> I had a most satisfactory account from Frances this morning of our 2 dear Children & a letter from Wm – In Speaking of the Oates whom he dislikes is the following paragraph wch you will allow does credit to his head & heart – 'They both render themselves so disagreeable by talking eternal nonsense wch by hearing constantly & being wearied makes me easily suppose how disagreeable I must have been to you & I shall never do it again'. Is this not pretty of Wm. his whole letter is so sincere and affectionate that I shall carefully preserve it for you. I wish you woud receive my money 25£ from I Humble & transmit it to me for my Cash is at a low ebb –

Young William was clearly practising his own epistolary style. His father sent the money, a banknote, but cut in half, one half in each of two separate letters. This was a practice recommended by the postal authorities because so much mail was waylaid by highwaymen.

Sarah was preparing a cottage for herself and William on the Townhill estate, and longed for him to be able to return to Yorkshire, if only the certificate could be granted. Cash problems were relative, however; their financial difficulties did not imply that Sarah proposed to sweep, cook and clean her house herself. She told William:

> I shall take possession of my house in a few days, as I find Nurse Reid will have no objection to remain with me till I am suited with a servant – There are fires on every day.

Cooler heads still counselled patience. Mr Duffield and young John Buck both thought William would be wise to remain in the south. If he returned to Yorkshire prematurely, explained Sarah, they thought that 'the prospect of any early certificate might make some small Creditors eager to molest you *whilst they can* & if Baild for one detainers might be lodged & others encouraged by the success of the first'.

Sarah had now been suffering the effects of her husband's disgrace for ten years. She was forty-four, her youth was lost and middle age was setting in:

> I wish you to bring me a pair of spectacles from Dollands in St Paul's Church Yd. Mrs Simpson's were delightful. They are called Dollands grand clearers the first degree and are mounted in Tortoiseshell price 7 or 8s.

In the cold light of January, 1805, the feverish activity and constant letter-writing seemed to have brought little result. Once the emotional and disturbing Mrs Whittaker was out of his sight, Mr Tipping had not done as he promised, the creditors and executors were adamant, and she was no nearer her goal. She found it humiliating that, when money was at stake, her adversaries could quite well withstand her affecting personal appeal. She bitterly regretted the letter of apology she had written to Thomas Tipping.

The criticism of the Whittakers' conduct over the sale of their household possessions was another blow to her pride. To crown it all, William had been calmly informed that his presence would not be necessary at the trial after all, and his 'services were dispensd with'. Sarah waxed sarcastic:

> Rather an extraordinary *denouement* after having detaind you so long in the country. To suppose a bare repayment of your Expences will be sufficient shows how much dependence may be placed on the assurances of these Honourable men – however I can only rejoice that your appearance in court will no longer be necessary and this Generosity will throw no impediment in the way of an affidavit wch I trust you will ere very long have the pleasure of making before a Master in Chancery –

The accusation of cheating during the sale of the Whittakers' household possessions ten years before distressed Sarah very much. Her halting explanations on the journey back to Bradford had brought a request from Mr Humble that she 'put down on paper' her own account of the episode.

She eagerly complied, and the story she told of her encounter with Mr Walker, the auctioneer, and her efforts to preserve a few of her chattels, was simple but eloquent:

> First, the Table Linnen – what we had at the farm was both good and plentiful, not one article of which I could be prevailed upon to take, though Walker urged me to select some, as a customary thing on such occasions – my refusal of it was because I was aware our future way of life would not require Damask and therefore prepared the more necessary accommodation of a few pair of callico sheets to which I have long been accustomed – he brought me also a set of tea china (a

wedding present from Mrs Duffield) and teaspoons and I was asked by him if I chose any little article of plate –

I had some wedding presents from my own friends which I valued and did not like to expose to a sale – these I also set aside with some books, the children's little chairs, and Sarah's feeding boat (she was then an infant) for the purpose of being valued that I might purchase these articles dear to me not from their intrinsic value but as connected with many affecting remembrances of happier days and friends, many of whom are now in the grave . . . The plate by order of the assignees was sent to Walkers all of which is specified in the enclosed valuation . . .

Being at Hart Hill many years after I found my friend Mr Simpson had with generous kindness got these things from Walker to whom he gave his note, to be answerable when called for, and insisted upon my taking them. I did so, but as Mr Simpson is now no more I was unwilling from motives of delicacy that Mrs Simpson be applied to and desired Miss White would give Walker directions to apply to me whenever the plate should be called for as I would be answerable for the amount.

Did the three friends that evening at Hart Hill invent the story of Mr Simpson's kind intervention? Did he really never settle the bills for Sarah's treasures with the auctioneer?

Sarah's unhappy story went on as she totted up the other items she had never paid for:

I am also charged with taking a Silver Tea-urn – we never possessed one – the furniture which has been mentioned was I think purchased by Mr Keysmar. The books I have since got valued the valuation 104 shillings – the other articles viz tea things and little chairs and table may perhaps be reckoned at seven pounds not undervalued – which will make the whole amount about thirty pounds which I pledge myself to make good from a little fund I have made for that purpose . . . in the

hope of discharging that and some other little debts at
Manchester as peculiarly my own – and as needful to
defray the expense of transporting myself and my two
children to America should the certificate be denied –
well knowing I could hope for no assistance from my
friends in executing a plan so contrary to their wishes –

The valuation which Sarah enclosed with this heartrending
report is dated 'Manch. Augt 9 1794' and is signed by 'M
Walker, Appraiser'. Mrs Whittaker's teapot, mustard pot,
and nine small spoons were valued at £7 4s; a 'Cadee' (caddy)
at £3 18s, and 2 'Scewers' (skewers) £1 18s, made a total of
£13.

Sarah had asked her Manchester friend Miss White to
remind Walker, the auctioneer, of the sale so many years
before:

> Walker told Miss White he perfectly remembered all
> that passd, that he never met with so conscientious a
> Lady, that there were many things I ought to have had
> but there was no overcoming my scruples & he wd if
> necessary make Oath on this before the Gentlemen.

After having to defend herself on every detail of the sale
ten years before, she abandoned her efforts to intercede
personally on William's behalf. She decided not to attend the
new meeting of creditors which had been called.

'My own opinion is that going to Manchester now might do
harm instead of good', she wrote. 'I had better remain quiet
at present – and serve as a corps de reserve a little while
hence.'

William regretted that his sister had 'taken it upon herself
to write to Mr Tipping', particularly after he had told her not
to do anything without his agreement. Other misguided
friends were also interfering:

> Miss Oates also talks of going to Manchester – I wish
> she do no mischeif [sic] there – I shd not wonder if she

were to debate the matter personally with the Tippings and the Hamiltons.

William obviously found the women's intervention embarrassing and wished they would keep out of it, however well-meant their intentions.

strange and unlookd for disappointment

A Frustrating Year, 1805

John William Buck, Caroline's son and Sarah's half-brother, was now a lively young man of twenty-five who, after protracted studies at Cambridge, was planning to study for the Bar at Lincolns Inn. Although he was twenty years younger than his sister, as a male and a university man he was considered to have a head start in wisdom and his advice was often sought.

John William Buck was also a man of property, who had inherited several farms at Denholme near Bradford from his father. His name appeared on a petition of 1803 in which nine Bradford persons of substance, including his stepfather Francis Duffield, Thomas Faber and himself, protested against the imposition of a rate on their property to pay for the street cleaning and lighting improvements introduced into the small town.

Although the distinction which his learning and wealth bestowed on him sometimes seemed to go to his head, Sarah was fond of her clever half-brother, and his presence meant more fun than she had enjoyed for years. They laughed, played music and talked late into the night about the young London professional men and their doings. John William Buck was also a useful role model for Sarah's young son William, who was now nearly fourteen. They both missed him sadly when he returned to London.

They had discussed young William's education seriously, and Sarah could not help twisting the knife gently when she wrote to her husband:

140

I have sent the money for Mr Esclin's bill last week and finding it was his intention for Wm to learn Mathematics the next half year and having consulted my Bro on the subject (not having you to apply to) who thought he had enough to learn at present – in my Letter to Mr Esclin I said I believed you did not wish William to begin with Mathematics until his future destination was more fixd.

Although Sarah yearned for her husband to come back to Yorkshire, Caroline, she explained, had persuaded her not to leave the comforts of Townhill for the cottage as yet. Nonetheless, the servants were sent scurrying across the wintry fields to keep the little house well aired:

I am not yet in my own House but as soon as I hear of your movements hitherwards I shall go and prepare my little Home for your reception – in the meantime it has daily fires – but Mrs D. thinks in my present anxious State I shd be quite melancholy to be there alone and the weather is too severe to be back and forward as I can in Summer.

In spite of her worries however, Sarah's letters bubbled along, full of news:

Mrs Duffield goes on charmingly – Mr Duffield complains a little of his toe – He was rather fatigued last night with assisting to elect an Usher for the Bradford School [Bradford Grammar School] a Mr Harrison from York is chosen a very nice pleasing young Man of about 25 whose Mother and Sisters mean to settle here – I am very glad you thought of the Oysters wch were very good and would have been still better had they not come by the Leicester Mail which shook them to a cream – but they were very fresh and well fed – I have got my Jewels wch were got out of the Casket into the bottom of my Trunk and wrote immediately to them at Bath.

141

Eventually, in the summer of 1805, all those daily fires were rewarded with the arrival of William from the south, and the couple settled down in their cottage. At least they were together again at last, and they confidently expected that the granting of William's certificate of discharge was only weeks away. They even decided on a short holiday and a 'change of air' in September, not conspicuously in Bath or Scarborough, but in a much quieter little spot – Gargrave, a pretty village beside the new Leeds-Liverpool canal.

Daniel Whittaker wrote to them there:

I see the Dividend is advertized for the 25th September but is not to be paid that day – can you tell me what was the amount of my aunts Mary and Sarah's claim as the debt has never been proved & as the Dividend is final and must be proved at this meeting as I wish it might be as it will be something for my Sisters.

Daniel's delicate prompting about the financial problems of the female Whittakers was a fresh reminder to the William of the way his whole family had been brought down by his business failure.

In the same month of September 1805, John William Buck was also having a recuperative holiday at Ramsgate after a shooting accident, and happily following some unusually pleasant medical advice:

My illness entirely proceeded from the bursting of the air Gun, and I never expected to be well again, but did not dare inform my Mother – on getting up to Town I went to one of the first Surgeons, who instantly perceivd what ailed me, as the Blow had prevented the secretion of Bile – he gave me something which removed the pain in a day or two, and said that the best thing would be for me to go down to the Sea, and likewise desird me to drink four or five glasses of wine after dinner. I have been uniformly on the amending hand and am now nearly as strong as ever –

Holidaymakers on the south coast that summer enjoyed themselves with an wary eye seawards through their spy-glasses. An invasion scare almost as severe as the desperate summer of 1803 had gripped the country, and Napoleon was rumoured to be massing his troops at Boulogne. In the Atlantic and the western approaches, the French and British fleets sailed and manoeuvred in the hunt for each other which culminated in the Battle of Trafalgar.

But by September, a month before Nelson's decisive British naval victory, London breathed more easily again as the invasion season passed. John William Buck no longer expected to have to return to his home county to join the Volunteers:

> If there is an end of all fear of invasion, it would be absurd to return home merely on account of Volunteering – You will see me the first week in November –

He also rashly added some views about his choice of career:

> Three or four reasons have induced me to study the Law. First and chief to get money (from which every terrestrial good springs) – Secondly that I need not marry a woman because she is rich. Thirdly that I shall have read as much Mathematics as I choose and then shall want something to do I certainly should have read more Mathematics with Mr Vince had he remained in Cambridge but considering my health it is better as it is. We have got through a great deal of maths, and it is now too late to wish, but if Lin. Coll. [Lincoln College] had existed ten years ago it would have been all the better for me.

John's candid view of his law career and the earlier account of his 'therapeutic' drinking seem to have caused a fluttering of disapproval in the maternal dovecote at Town-hill. It was not long before he had to write hastily to his sister again, hoping she might placate a shocked Caroline:

143

My Mother seems to think my draughts rather too frequent – but young eagles must have food.

John usually sprinkled his letters lavishly with literary allusions, but on this occasion, his Shakespearean memory was slightly faulty – in *The Merry Wives of Windsor* it was young ravens which required sustenance. He went on with a Biblical flourish:

> Now if you can only convince her that the Money is not absolutely thrown away you will do me a kindness – who can handle pitch and not be defiled? Who can live amongst the Mammonite Bradfordians and not be tinged with their idolatry?
>
> Mr Balme and myself had a snug dinner at his home – he informs me that he has been at Bradford lately and in particular mentioned how well you and my Mother lookd – I smuggld a jar of Ginger which is just gone off by the Waggon as a present to my Father –

As the September of 1805 advanced, they all scanned the newspapers anxiously for news of the signing of William's certificate of discharge. There was still an ominous silence from Mr Tipping and his advisers and cronies. John wrote that 'As Mr Whittaker resides without molestation at Bradford, it seems as though their intentions are good respecting the signing of the certificate – I have looked constantly in the papers for it'.

The chill of November brought disappointment to the Whittakers. The promises of a September certificate were not fulfilled, and William's position in Bradford remained precarious. He could not engage in business, and had no way of earning a living without risking molestation by his still vengeful creditors.

Nearly a whole year had gone by since Sarah's interview with Mr Tipping, and nothing had yet been settled. She wrote a resentfully pathetic letter to the lawyer, Mr Eccles, of such interminable length, with so many deletions and repetitions, that probably it is only the first draft which survives in her papers. She pleaded to know 'some cause for my strange and unlookd for disappointment', and why Mr Tipping refused 'to fulfil those hopes upon wch I have for a whole year relied with the most implicit confidence'.

She rehearsed the whole protracted story yet again – the apparent relenting of Mr Tipping, the 'unexpected resistance of Mr. Greg', the stipulation that a new meeting of creditors be called, the necessary appointment of new commissioners in bankruptcy and the opportunity this gave for a new batch of creditors to prove their debts. Two of these, Mrs Hamilton and Mr Crane, were 'feared to be inexorable'. Sarah always seemed to be specially wounded when a woman opposed her:

> Of Mrs Hamilton's signature I believe we must utterly despair and of Mr Crane's we are Equally Hopeless – That a Woman should not feel for a Woman in my circumstances is most incomprehensible, and that a Mortal Man on the Verge of Eternity shd be unforgiving is equally surprizing –

She defended herself once more against Mr Greg's accusation over the valuables spirited from the auction sale, and insisted that she was not capable of such 'sordid meanness'.

The only hope of bending the adamant Mrs Hamilton and Mr Crane to signing the agreement appeared to lie in Mr Touchett, a Manchester manufacturer, who was thought to have some influence on them. Sarah wrote wearily to her friend Mrs Simpson of Hart Hill to ask again for her help:

> Your kind Letter, my dear Friend, found me in a deep dejection wch for ought I see is likely to be long my portion – we hear nothing the least encouraging from Manchester, and in consequence Mr Whittaker is making his arrangements for again leaving the Kingdom, and taking what I fear will be a final adieu of his Wife and Family –

145

The only possible chance in our Favor is procuring the signatures of Mrs Hamilton and Mr Crane through Mr Touchett's good offices – Mr Tipping insists on all signing before he will – I hope Mr Touchett will benevolently exert his interest in our behalf and will accept the distressful emergency of the situation.

Sadly, Mr Touchett either did not choose to intervene or was unsuccessful. As the weeks went on, it became clear to William that his hopes of being granted his certificate of discharge were not going to be realised. He decided that he had no choice but to return to America the following spring (1806). He and Sarah were plunged further into gloom.

Life for the rest of the family had to go on, however, and young William, their son, was now growing up. He had written to his mother from school 'expressing a wish for Theological Studies' or as he put it 'to read an account of the the different religions of the world'.

Sarah hastily wrote to Mr Esclin, the schoolmaster:

. . . you will probably agree with me that he had better be well informed as to the Evidences of Christianity in general than bewilder himself with all the various tenets – I have therefore delayed complying with his request to point him out proper Books on the subject, knowing he is in much better hands if you would have the goodness to direct his studies.

The family obviously discussed young William's programme at length, and decided what subjects the boy would study. John Buck expressed his usual refreshingly forthright opinions about his nephew's schooling:

Your son Billy sent me a long letter a day or two ago, I suppose thinking it right to keep up a connection with his old Uncle, as there is no knowing what may happen – the poor lad seems to be workd very hard, and as Johnson said of the Scotch Universities, to have a mouthful of everything and a bellyful of nothing.

146

John Buck had the heartfelt views of experience on language studies, which he was happy to pass on:

> Charles [Faber] arrived on Friday night – he says that Wm. has grown a very fine lad. If Mr W and you intend following the plan of education we talked of when I was at Bradford, pray don't let him at present learn French – Latin, Greek and English are in my opinion as many languages as his head will carry at once.
>
> But if you think not, pray try yourself and begin the Greek, Latin and German grammars, and I think in a week's time you will be able to appreciate the difficulty of learning three languages at once.

John ideas on general reading are typical of his day. They were liberal – so long as the boy was not seduced into wasting his time with fiction:

> Let Wm read anything he chooses – novels excepted, he may take what books he can find at Townhill. It is surprising what information a boy gains by desultory reading, and he will have sufficient of system at school – but novels are Midianitish [idolatrous] books. Has he got a Murray's grammar? If he hasn't I will give him one.

John was already drafting important legal documents for his friends, and described his work with his usual candour:

> I have at length got rid of Mrs Broadhurst's marriage writings which hung like a millstone round the neck of my conscience, but by a desperate effort I ordered a pennyworth of brown paper and sent them off to Bath forthwith.
>
> Tell my Mother the 100£ came safe to hand and that Dyneley has written to me. Most certainly he will not leave The Lion to live with Mrs Dyneley – he may say with his great prototype Bardolph 'it is a life I have desird, I will thrive'.

How necessary the marriage settlements were had already been demonstrated in Sarah's case, and his story of the

147

Dyneleys was another reminder of the fragile security of women. The errant and probably bibulous Mr Dyneley seems to have resembled Shakespeare's red-nosed Bardolph in his fondness for the tapster's role.

The expenses of his life as a law student were beginning to trouble John's conscience, as Francis Duffield, his stepfather, seems to have been providing his funds at this period. He decided, rather reluctantly, to make a present of his horse to Mr Duffield's young nephew Francis – who was also in London – as a placatory move, and perhaps also as a hint to the provincials that London was very costly for a student:

> My Mother would mention my having made a present of the little Horse to Francis – its value just at present would have been very acceptable to me, but as my Father will be at a considerable expence when I go to a special pleader, I thought it proper to pay this commission to his nephew. For indeed the poor lad has seldom a shilling in his pocket, and therefore is precluded from slipping into Dukes or Nicholas Mason's of an evening to take a glass with his peers –

The 'special pleader' was a barrister who would instruct the student lawyer in the complicated techniques of civil cases. Before the reforms effected in the 1850s Common Law Procedure Acts, writs, replies, defences and counterclaims had to be presented in a technically correct manner, by 'special pleas', or the case would not be heard.

Economy was to be John's watchword, he assured Sarah, with the hope that she would pass the message on to his mother and stepfather. At this period, personal visits to Townhill seem to have been necessary when he needed his funds topped up:

> Charles says that my Mother and Father have some intentions of coming up to Town this spring – it gives me pleasure to hear it, as I certainly shall not set foot

in Yorks this year of our Lord, and in order to be better able to do this, I shall neither keep Man nor Horse –

But the next time he wrote to his sister, John had taken up his social round again with enthusiasm. 'In great haste', he wrote, 'I am going to make an Idle Evening by dining out at Mahommed's with a party of young Lawyers – the Dinner is to consist entirely of Indian dishes after which Sherbet, though I hope with a little "anding" [addition], will moisten palates dried by fragrant fumes of the Eastern Hokkah [hookah].'

And soon afterwards, he was able to make an expansive gesture to his sister and brother-in-law for their son's education, his own financial position miraculously improved. Very likely, at the age of twenty-five, he had taken control of his trust funds.

Mr Barmby, the headmaster of Bradford Grammar School, had been consulted. He described young William as a 'fine lad' who would become a 'good scholar both from his diligence and his abilities'. The family had therefore decided that William 'should be brought up to a profession', as there were no funds to set him up in business, and it would be necessary for him to earn his living in a respectable manner. John had 'turned the matter over', and intended to help his nephew with more than mere advice.

With tongue slightly in cheek, perhaps smarting over scathing views of lawyers from an embittered William Whittaker senior, John described the status of a professional man as a relatively obscure and lowly one, compared with that of the gentleman or the man of affairs. His own busy and profitable professional life he kindly did not compare with that of his brother-in-law. Clearly the money which had been invested in his career had not all been wasted on wining and dining:

You may reckon on me as debtor to the use of William's education of 300£ which I shall set in the Funds by instalments and will send you the receipts. As

149

my expences are now very limited I shall so be able to
do this that the interest will amount to near a hundred
pounds more. You need not be under any apprehension
on this head, as I live within my income and have money
beforehand. I only mention 300£ for should I get
married, it might not be in my power to do more – but
with what you are able to add, there would be a
considerable surplus after paying his Lin Coll [Lincoln
College] expences.

Young William was to follow a similar path to that of his
uncle – mathematics at Cambridge, followed by training for
the Bar. John could help further:

I likewise should be able two years before his entry
to put him into such a method of reading mathematics
as would give him advantages superior to most young
men, the consequence of which ought to be a fellowship,
and that always leads to something better – To be sure
that plan does not promise wealth and splendour, but it
most certainly leads to competence, content, a 'cleanly
and a quiet privacy' – a family need not idolize Trade –

John's last remark probably reflects ambivalent attitudes
among the top Bradford families towards the rising wealth of
the millowners. They were accustomed to hearing scornful
reports of the brash and even uncouth manners of the
nouveaux riches of their day, and yet envy was probably never
far away. The smell of new money was enough to make some
people 'idolize trade'. As in every era, business was
acceptable enough if it led to wealth, when social advantages
followed.

But the family had also seen the effects of 'trade' on
William Whittaker's life, and those of friends who had been
'unfortunate'. The professions, although not enjoying the
prestige they have today, at least did not involve the dizzying
rises and desperate falls of business life. Finding his feet as
a lawyer, John, with 'I told you so' pride, added a triumphant
last word to what was probably a regular family debate.

like some Solitary Ghost

Parting, 1806

For over a decade of war the cotton merchants had struggled to sell and be paid. They had made endless costly mistakes – suffering risky or impossible forecasting of demand, overstocking, shortages or dumping, as the fortunes of sea war shifted. They had suffered the loss of their ships to French privateers which harried Caribbean waters, and the addition of Spain and her colonies to the French side had meant that more ports were hostile to Britain. There was regular bad news of ships and cargoes. Daniel Whittaker noted a typical avalanche of disaster when he wrote to William in the autumn of 1805:

> Your letter for New York is forwarded per William Penn. The Bostock of this Port, 2 Ships for London, 1 for Bristol, 1 for Greenock, being 5 of the Amern [American] Fleet, are taken and carrd. into Cuba.

After the crucial Battle of Trafalgar, however, a second defeat of the French fleet at Occa Bay off Santo Domingo really put paid to the sea war in the Caribbean. The French alliance grew unpopular in Spain and its colonies.

On the mainland of Europe, Bonaparte's Grand Army swept eastwards, defeating Britain's allies, Austria and Russia, at the battle of Austerlitz in December 1805. This blow caused William Pitt to ask Lady Hester Stanhope to 'roll up the map of Europe'. A month later Pitt died, leaving Britain and her allies in disarray and the outlook in Europe bleak.

151

It was the effect on trade of the shifting military alliances which had the most impact on businessmen. In Liverpool, reported William's brother Daniel, 'the immediate prospect of war with Prussia has caused a general stagnation and alarm here among the German houses'.

Prussia, which had been courted as an ally by both sides in the conflict between Britain and France, had entered the war on the side of the French early in 1806, and had barred the use of its North German ports to its former ally. The British had retaliated by seizing a large number of Prussian ships on the high seas. Later in the same year, the Prussians changed sides again and were to suffer the contempt of Bonaparte and his revenge at the battles of Jena and Auerstadt.

In the spring of 1806 there seemed to be real prospects of peace with Napoleon, or at least a stalemate, with Britain ruling the seas and the French Emperor the continent of Europe. For the business people who traded with the West Indies and the United States, it looked as though their ships might at last be able to operate unimpeded.

In March 1806, Michael Humble, who was now the owner of Shooters Hill, a splendid country estate at Rossington near Doncaster, sent Sarah £200 to help William travel across the Atlantic again. His letter included an optimistic view of what might be achieved in the Caribbean area, certainly to a citizen of the United States like William, now that the British navy had completed its defeat of the French and Spanish fleets, and the busy and useful port of Havana was friendly once more. The many prizes which the French had escorted to Havana during the previous year were probably in Mr Humble's mind as he wrote:

> Cuba just now offers to the citizens of the United States a fair opportunity of uncommon advantage from the purchase of foreign ships and goods etc – my opinion is no time should be lost – to arrive there in the hottest season would surely be impolatick at least

His touch of impatience with William was characteristic. However, for his next transatlantic trip, William was planning something different from the precarious and lonely life of an agent. He had told everyone, including Mr Humble, that he was 'in honour bound' to return to Cuba, whether he was granted his certificate of discharge or not. He had engaged himself, he had assured them, with an attempt at dignity, in an enterprise to found a distillery at Matanzas. Michael Humble, always sharp and practical, professed himself surprised that William had delayed so long if indeed his distillery plans were serious.

'I imagine', he wrote pointedly, 'that the Stills have got to Cuba 12 months ago at least. I hope on his arrival he does not find the scheme abandoned as from his reports to me the prospects seemd very flattering.'

Mr Humble assured Sarah that:

> as to my £200 it is with you my dear Mrs W to do as you see most for your interest and happiness – the same motive at present exists which at first actuated us viz the making of your mind easy by a conviction that your Husband was doing something to provide for himself and perhaps raising a surplus for his family which I sincerely hope and trust will be the case.

Mr Humble's pious hopes filled much of his letter, but he also gave her news of London friends and relatives. 'Your brother dined with me yesterday', he informed her, and 'Mr Todd is wonderfully well'.

At length there was no more time left. The season for sailing was already advanced. William arranged his passage and set out for Liverpool on the 23rd May 1806, after an anguished parting with his wife and children. Sarah was inconsolable. She was now forty-six, and it seemed for the second time that she would lose her husband for ever. On the Sunday morning after he left, she sat down to write to him. At least the start of his journey had been propitious and comfortable:

You are now my dearest Willm. I trust safely arrived at Liverpool – as I had the satisfaction of hearing by Mr Vincent that you were in time for the Mail and found one place ready to receive which I was glad of as you would travel in that more speedily and pleasantly than in the Heavy Coach.

Her description of the hours after their parting is painful:

And now for the little journal of those you left behind. I returned to bed after your departure as I seemed to have no exertion for a walk to Spink Well. After our melancholy Breakfast was over and poor Wm despatched to school, I wandered about our Garden like some Solitary Ghost, and sat down on a seat till I could bear it no longer. I then had recourse to the Bible for consolation and accidentally opened it to the 55th Psalm. This was also too affecting and too applicable.

I closed the volume and determined to betake myself to active employment wch succeeded rather better, tho every drawer and closet brought some moments of departed Happiness –

Caroline Duffield, acutely aware of her friend's distress, was awaiting her chance to provide a diversion:

from this employ I was relieved by Mrs Duffield about 11 o'clock, who brought her Work to sit the morning with me. She wanted me to accompany her in the afternoon in the Chaise to Calverley, but you may imagine that was the last place I shd wish to go. She found Mrs Faber downstairs but seemed to think her in a very precarious state.

It seemed a long time since the happy days of their youth which the two friends had passed at Calverley Vicarage. Sarah could not face it. Her Saturday had been just as cheerless, although she and the children had tried to continue their routine:

Madame Serelly had a bad cold yesterday and sent her excuses for not calling on me and requesting that I would go and sit with her a while. I declined this as you may imagine. I wonder she could think I shd do otherwise. We did not neglect to water the garden last night in which our whole Trio was diligently employed and we shall continue to do so with a sort of religious punctuality –

She revealed her true feelings over William's possibly harebrained plans in a sharper and more furious sentence than she normally allowed herself:

My constant wish and *only hope* is that you may never engage in this odious distillery – if you do I shall never expect to see you again in this world. In the meanwhile I think of our dear little Cottage and what a Desert it is become to me tho Gay Blooming and Cheerful to everyone else.

She sent a book to William with her letter, 'the little Almanac which you left behind'. The bearer of both was Mr Vincent, Francis Duffield's nephew, who was setting out for a visit to Liverpool. He had called on Sarah for some advice and to arrange the plan of his journey:

I advised him by all means to go to the Theatre in the evening whch he means to do, and will get as far as Littleborough this Evening. He means to be absent as long as his money (10 Guineas) lasts – I have conscientiously sent the Almanac supposing you designed it should accompany you, but if not return it and also send me one of yr. *grey locks* wch I lamented I had not made sure of before you went.

The idea of the grey hair brought tears to Sarah's eyes once more. She was very conscious of her pathetic situation. But in spite of her depression, she could hardly contain her curiosity to know what was being said in Liverpool:

155

How interesting will this day's conversation between you and DW [Daniel Whittaker] be to me – How I wish I could hear it and your interview with Miss White and Mr Spear – Of both I beg you to send me a very particular account and write by the *post* as Mr Vincent will, if a great Oeconomist, be absent perhaps a forthnight.

On Sunday, as she took up her pen, she was still inclined to seek solitude:

Wm. is gone to Church with Mrs Duffield, and desird his best love. I am more disposed to perform my Sunday duties in private and fervently pray for our speedy reunion – Mrs Dean called yesterday but was not admitted as I had previously told Hannah I did not wish to see anyone

Four days later she wrote again. William's ship had been delayed, not unexpectedly, awaiting a fair wind:

I fear the East Wind has now taken leave for some time the lack will either detain you at Liverpool or occasion you a very tedious voyage. At all events, I think you will not depart so soon as Sunday, as *my experience* in maritime affairs teaches me that Captains seldom set out so soon as they talk of doing –

Naturally she regretted not having travelled to Liverpool with him, and entreated him to write as long as he was within reach of the post:

I do not feel as though we were quite separate, tho God knows at times desolate enough. I thought a week ago that when our separation was over I shd feel more at ease and now wd gladly purchase even the pain of *another farewell*! so deceitful the Heart and so blind the Judgment we form of our feelings.

The protracted leave-taking became something of a trial as May turned into June. Sarah wrote again and again:

> This is the last letter you receive from me in England – God bless you my dear Husband, grant fair winds and a prosperous voyage, a Healthy and Short sojourn at New York and a happy and speedy return – as for me, I will endeavour to Hope again and fortify my Heart and my Head as much as possible both to support myself under this heavy trial and to perform those duties towards your Children whch unhappily now devolve entirely on me.

Before long, she 'bitterly repented' not accompanying William to Liverpool. He had written to say he planned definitely to return to England if he found the distillery plan abandoned. The newspapers were full of the continued friction between Britain and America. The Americans insisted on their rights as neutrals to trade with French ports, and the British, now rulers of the seas, were even more determined to prevent them. Sarah grasped at any possibility of stopping William:

> Don't you think there is now a great likelihood of an American War? and that your going is still more ineligible?

In spite of her feelings, Sarah did not fill all her long letters with lamentation. She drew lively pictures of the summer in Bradford, her garden and the constant comings and goings of visitors. Despite herself, she was drawn into sociability:

> The Stovins are expected at Townhill next Saturday – Mrs Shores visit is delayed on account of a horse falling ill wch I am glad of – as I shall perhaps be more disposed to receive pleasure from her Society – Our Lilacs and Laburnums are now in full beauty and on Monday the Fly Orchis began to blow and now exhibits 2 Mimic Insects –

Mr Walter Stott calld at Townhill today and had intended calling here – was much surprized to find you gone and sorry he did not see you first, as it might have been in his power to assist you with introductory letters, as he understood by Mr Humble you are bound for Havana. Mr and Mrs Stott I fancy do not mean to establish themselves at Eccleshill for the present – it is now said they will live with Mr Simons for a few years till his debts are paid off –

Mr Stott, a Bradford businessman who clearly had his own debt problems, had made a carefully belated attempt to offer some introductions in Cuba. Vague helpfulness sounded polite but did not involve Mr Stott too closely.

Young William was enjoyable company for his mother during that summer. He had 'his schoolfellows Rand and Atkinson to Tea' one day, and looked after his pets. Sarah wrote:

William's Rabbit has produced Young – but how many we cannot yet ascertain – we had an odd sort of Robbery the other Day – somebody entered the passage door (the other being barrd) and took a ½ lb of butter and 2 oatcakes leaving three Silver Spoons 2 loaves and piece of cheese wch were just by and one wd have though a more valuable prize – wch made us first suspect the Thief to be a Dog – but in eating or carrying away the Butter a Dog wd have left some marks and all was clean and trackless –

In a few days the rabbits had been counted and she was again writing about their visitors and the garden:

On Sunday morning when I gave Wm a clean shirt I found had by mistake put 2 of yr best ruffled ones amongst his, and these pursuing east winds now determine me to send them – our dear Boy is at school and very happy with his ten young Rabbits – a large party drank Tea at Townhill yesterday. I declined going

– it was a Holiday and I felt more inclined to spend it with Wm at Home.

It was Heavy and Incessant Rain all day and this morning sunshine makes the garden look so gay and thriving it wd delight you to see it – The Stovins came last Saturday and left on Tuesday morning. Theo looks most dreadfully and Miss Stovin is much altered – 'th'ould lass is the best of the bunch'.

Sarah enjoyed adding a few Yorkshire-isms to her elegant phrases. The plain-speaking Stovins were 'much piqued', she added, because they expected Henry Faber to call on them to thank Mrs Stovin for a favour, but 'nowt o'th sort'.

Being dependent on friends and relatives for transport was galling. Her daughter Sarah was at school in Bath with a daughter of the Humbles, but 'There is no possibility of dear Sally [Sarah] coming home this summer, as I find Susan Humble does not come home'.

But ways and means were found in the end, through kind friends' help. Her mother joyfully wrote at the end of June, after William had finally sailed for New York:

You will I am sure rejoice to hear that my Dear Girl arrived home late on Monday last. I went down to the Coach to receive her, and the meeting was so joyful that she could only express it with her Tears which were plentifully shed. Mrs. Belcher had kindly received her at Manchester and forwarded her in company with Mr and Mrs Surr from thence – she has brought a cough with her and looks thin but in other aspects I think her much improved.

Comings and goings increased all through June as the season for paying summer holiday visits advanced. Margaret Humble, Mr Humble's sister, came to stay with Sarah, the Duffields went to take the waters at Harrogate and Francis Duffield's nephew Mr Vincent came back from Liverpool. The young man was 'much delighted with his trip. He says he was never so happy in his life'.

Young Mr Vincent had also become inclined to boast after experiencing the stimulating atmosphere of a great international port, and aroused consternation at the Townhill dinner table:

> Mr Vincent is under a serious temptation to accompany you – indeed it wd be impossible either without means or permission – Miss Duffield dined at Townhill Today and by way of joke her Bro mentioned that 'Francis is going to America' wch excited such a torrent of Tears and Displeasure – that I believe he repented his merriment – I daresay she is afraid you will endeavour to tice her Nephew away, and shd he go that wd be the good-natured construction of evryone.

Margaret Humble took young William to Halifax for the day in her chaise so that he could visit some old schoolfriends. The boy was obviously a favourite of the Humbles and when Mr Humble came to collect his sister they took him off with them to Shooters Hill for a summer holiday.

The cure at Harrogate was not a success, and the Duffields returned disappointed. The friends of long ago were all beginning to feel their age:

> The Crescent water has not agreed with Mrs Duffield – she has sent a letter saying they return home tomorrow – she is anxious about her Sister – she went to Bolton Abbey but was so fatigued with the journey that she was very ill on getting there.

Michael Humble, 'who we all know is no keeper of secrets', wrote Sarah dryly, told her that 'Noel Stott was for arresting his Bro since the old woman died'. The beleaguered Stott family obviously had similar problems to the Whittakers:

> Mr Humble with some difficulty persuaded W.S. [Walter Stott] to abandon his intention of going abroad – he gave him for a Toast the afternoon he was here

'Your Friends in Trinidad and may you never see them
again' – and I understand he promised Mr Humble he
would not.

It must have seemed to Sarah that everyone who talked of
going to the West Indies except her husband was only too
easily dissuaded. Was he braver, or simply more obstinate?
She continued with her tales about their life in Bradford –
perhaps to make William think about what he was missing.
That summer his daughter was also growing up:

> Sarah has had the pleasure of seeing her rose Tree in
> full beauty as are the moss Roses, and to pick some
> cherries from the little Tree. I yesterday stocked
> William's garden with the cucumber plants Ezekiel
> raised – Master Sturges has got his two older Rabbits
> and the others occupy Mrs Speight's catt House for wch
> he has to pay Tythe of his young ones – Sarah and the
> ass are great cronies. She rides it daily and frequently
> has Miss Jones on Mossman as whipper in – Mad.
> Serelly speaks well of Sarah's progress in French wch
> she says she translates very well but does not pronounce
> as well as her Bro. She has brought some beautiful
> Drawings and is much improved on the harpsichord.

The summer jaunts and visits continued – everyone in the
country seemed to be bowling along the roads in post-chaises
or trundling in the heavy coaches, avid to see friends and
relatives after the long and tedious winter months.

The Fabers went to the Lakes. Sarah took her daughter to
stay with the Humbles at Shooters Hill. She and young
William were to return by the first week of August, leaving
young Sarah to be escorted back to school at Bath with the
Humbles. At Doncaster, she learned of a highly important
piece of information, which 'impatient to communicate good
news my dear William', she passed on rather cryptically to
her husband, who was by now halfway across the Atlantic:

161

I hasten to inform you of an Act of Parliament recently passed wch will enable a Dear Friend of ours, (you will guess who) to revisit his Country and Family whenever he chooses. It is passed in favor of uncertificated Bankrupts and tho it allows Creditors to attach property, prevents them from any Power over the persons of their Debtors – I am desirous you should be empowered to communicate this to our Friend before he quits New York in the Hope it may induce him *immediately* to return to England. I saw something of the kind in the papers a few weeks ago but did not know it had actually passed until this morning when Mr Humble arrived from L [Liverpool] – Mr Humble saw Mr Darke of Liverpool whose Sons have been unfortunate – he was rejoicing and says it might be made a purpose for his poor Lads.

Young John Buck was also planning a summer visit to Townhill. He had written from 2 Lincolns Inn Fields ('you will see I am at Shop'), weary of London, and pining, rather affectedly, for country air:

I shall be able to quit this place about the beginning of August – The sight of our Ings [fields] full of Fog will appear to me as the child that in one act starts into manhood in The Winter's Tale. I don't know whether you have experienced this sensation, but after being all spring and summer 'in populous city pent' and having no intermediate stages of progressive gestation to fix the attention, the corn and fruits of different kinds seem to be produced all at once by a kind of magic – indeed I sicken for the country – by the by, it was lucky your bills was paid, I did not know as much of these matters as I do now, having had to draw up some law proceedings on a similar case.

John's legal knowledge now included the intricacies of bankruptcy, and he was later to become a celebrated specialist in bankruptcy cases. Possibly his half-sister's misfortunes had developed his own interest in the subject.

From the Humbles' country house at Shooters Hill, Sarah wrote on, telling her husband all about the summer's events:

> Sally and I arrived here on Monday and left our friends at the great House [Townhill] meditating another jaunt as soon as their Hay should be achieved – Mrs. D. [Duffield] tells me J.B. [John Buck] preparatory to arrival has sent an Oyster barrel full of Boot Top powder – so he means to be a very Beau-ish counsellor.

She was relieved and delighted to discover that young William had enjoyed his stay immensely. The summer holiday seems to have been a successful mixture of fun and duties. He was growing up fast, and assuming his father's chivalrous manners, wrote Sarah fondly:

> I found William looking extremely well and you wd be entertained to see what a flirtation is carried on between him and Harriet Humble. I assure you he has profited not a little by yr instructions and is quite the Galant Man – I don't know how he will relish the Barmby Parrot and Drum on his return –

Mr Barmby, the grammar school master, might not have been quite so pleased to hear how Mrs Whittaker described his methods. She went on:

> He [William] is much improved in Swimming since he came by daily practice in the pond, and he is going this afternoon with Mr Humble to shoot Rabbits and Wood Pigeons. He looks extremely well tho much sunburnt and is all alive and active – he keeps school in a morning and instructs Master Humble in writing and Latin exercises – devotes an Hour or more to his Uncle's Task and the rest of the day is devoted to Amusement and sometimes a Dance finishes off the Evening – when Harriet is sometimes coquettish enough to be previously engaged –

J.B. will be at Townhill the first week in August,
where I shall also journey as soon as the Bath party are
off – Dear Sally [Sarah] has still a little Cough, but it
mends daily wch in part I attribute to plenty of
Strawberries wch she has here – I never saw such
profusion anywhere.

Some tempers and dispositions are very loath to give up a point

A Hurtful Accusation, 1806

Throughout the sunny days of spring and summer 1806, and the diversions of that eventful season, Sarah adjusted to her husband's departure, and her natural good spirits re-asserted themselves. But there was one shadow over her mind which would not dissipate. In fact it grew steadily darker and more ominous.

During Miss Margaret Humble's visit in June, one topic had continually recurred. She had told Sarah that her brother Michael Humble was still extremely angry about £500 which he said William had misappropriated ten years earlier, soon after he arrived in Charleston. Although he had been allowed to draw this sum, it had been intended for the purchase of cotton. Mr Humble apparently took the view that William had applied this money to wild and ill-considered schemes of his own.

Sarah was appalled, and had already urged William as a matter of great importance to see Michael Humble in Liverpool before he sailed for New York, 'in wch case you will be able to explain that misunderstanding wch has caused us all so much uneasiness'.

Another long conversation with Margaret Humble made Sarah even more apprehensive. Surely Mr Humble was mistaken, and why was he making such an accusation so long after the event? William had always behaved with perfect integrity – he must have failed to explain his actions clearly. She wrote again, insistently, to her husband:

I am more than ever desirous that you should enter into an explanation with Mr Humble respecting the 500L – how his original mistake arose I cannot divine but I find he is more confirmed in it by our silence.

Sarah had opened her private chest of documents and searched them for letters to prove William's innocence to Michael Humble's sister:

I showd Margaret all the papers yesterday and she immediately understood the whole and wonders how her Bro coud make the mistake – Mr Duffield has also explained it and now I feel easier than I did – but shall not be entirely satisfied until Mr Humble is also –

John Buck was asked for his view of the disquieting grumbles from the Humble camp, and replied to his half-sister with characteristic impatience:

All that Mic Humble said to me respecting Mr W's affairs was giving me some tiresome account of his (Mr W) advancing some money on goods or I do not know what, not understanding these matters – and moreover the whole set of them kept it up so handsomely that I am sure my memory of it the next morning was a complete vacuum –

A few days later, the subject was raised yet again, and Sarah began to feel panicky. She wrote to William:

Mr Humble sees your drawing the Bill originally in so heinous a light and I wish Mr Duffield had been home, as the opinion of some Mercantile Man wd have more weight than anything I can urge in extenuation.

Michael Humble's anger seemed to be directed solely at Sarah's husband. In spite of his resentment, which as it turned out, seemed to have rankled since William's ill-fated voyages of 1796, his friendship and affection for Sarah and her children did not waver. During the summer of 1806, Mr

Humble and his sister continued to include Sarah in their summer visiting programme, took young William to Doncaster for his summer holiday, and had welcomed her and young Sally to Shooters Hill. He had also sent her £200, with a carefully worded letter.

Sarah, however, naturally felt keenly this rumbling disapproval of her husband, which was now erupting so unexpectedly and so fiercely. The attack on William's integrity must be fought. Although she had been thoroughly chastened after her last abortive effort to influence a 'mercantile man', Mr Tipping, she decided to have it out with Mr Humble when he came to collect Margaret and young William to take them to Shooters Hill.

The meeting was a difficult one and, dismayed and frightened after it, she wrote a blow-by-blow account of the conversation for William and Daniel, 'whilst still fresh in my memory'. Her pen brings to life that contentious scene between two determined people, which had occurred while the unsuspecting William Whittaker was still in Liverpool awaiting his passage to New York.

At first the wary Mr Humble had been unwilling even to broach the subject. It would only be painful, he said, and William had already owned he had done wrong. Mr Humble had shaken hands at his parting for America, and sincerely forgiven him, 'though he must ever think his conduct had been extremely wrong and even dishonourable in that business'.

Sarah would not accept that. William, she said, had only done wrong 'in so far as deviating from his instructions, he had taken an undue liberty with the House at Liverpool'.

As to forgiveness, she said stoutly, Mr Humble in fact owed it to William for injuring him by his misconceptions and misrepresentations. She had letters and papers to prove that William had sent property to Charleston to reimburse Mr Humble, and as the goods were insured, he considered being out of the money for a few months was the only inconvenience Mr Humble had suffered.

Michael Humble pounced on this. Aha! he riposted with a flourish:

The goods coud only be insured from the Dangers of Sea and Capture, but who coud insure him from the dangers of bad and unfortunate speculation?

The money Mr W took out with him was already gone in some such way, and by drawing this Bill he woud risk 500L more of other people's money – for wch Mr. H. woud be entirely responsible, having guaranteed his partners that the cd [credit] given Mr W coud only be used for the purpose of shipping Cotton and by no means for entering on such a speculative and uncertain trade as that between Charleston and Havannah was well known to be –

In short, a Man who woud draw a Bill under such circumstances woud not scruple keeping it as long as it was convenient.

Sarah counter-attacked. She showed Mr Humble William's first letter describing his problems in Charleston, 'explaining all his inducements to the step and the Idle and expensive life he must otherwise continue, the advice of Messrs Pippin and McLeod, the proposal to remit all possible effects to Charleston for the purpose of repaying, and that the effects were sent'.

She showed Mr Humble a sheaf of papers, and an account from Mr Fraser, William's former business associate. Mr Humble dismissed this as worthless – 'a mere trading account'. It was 'extraordinary', he said, that there was no proof from Mr Fraser that goods were sent for the purpose of repaying him. He thought William should obtain a copy of any letter referring to the matter from Mr Fraser. Sarah resisted this stoutly because, as Michael Humble well knew, William had quarrelled with Mr Fraser.

Mr Humble, she said, 'must know that from Mr. W's present situation with the Frasers that he woud neither ask nor woud they give any favor and as to any copy of letters, were Mr W capable of the conduct Mr H imputes to him, he wd also be capable of fabricating any Letter wch woud answer his purpose'.

As the protagonists stopped to draw breath, Sarah's servant Hannah threw open the door and announced 'Mr Whittaker!'.

'In the surprize of the moment', continued Sarah, 'I ran to receive my Husband and had nearly embraced a stranger – a gentleman of the same name who lives here and transacts business with Mr H. He stayed till bedtime and breakfasted here next morning when W Stott came and they all went off together.'

When Mr Humble returned 'to a late dinner', Sarah warmed to her subject again. How could he believe, she said passionately, that William could 'premeditatingly injure the only friend who in his greatest necessity had stepped forward to help him? The Honest Indignation his letters now expressed in being suspected of so foul a crime (one that might stamp him equally knave and fool) would of itself be to me convincing proof of his integrity'.

The shaky logic of this argument signally failed to impress Mr Humble. He unkindly reminded Sarah of William's bankruptcy. Sarah said that that had been entirely different. Because 'a whole Family' depended on his efforts, he had been led on 'step by step to go to lengths and Hazards to wch his own interest alone woud never have tempted him, and now is the sacrifice for all'.

Mr Humble, becoming impatient, shifted his ground. He thought Mr Madan, William's proposed partner in the distillery plan, had been badly treated. He fired questions at Sarah. Why had William not gone back to New York earlier? Sarah replied that he could not know whether the distillery was to go ahead until he got there. Why had he not written, then, instead of wasting money? Because he had promised to go, and felt in honour bound to return. And how had he taken his capital out? Daniel had arranged it, and Sarah had wanted him to have £200 of her savings – but instead, knowing she

169

had expenses with young William's education, he insisted she keep £100 of his own.

Sarah said William was incapable of forming a plan to 'entrap anyone, and that it hurt my mind not a little that Mr W shoud leave England with the painful and irritating impression that he was suspected of such conduct – in addition to those griefs which must be supposed of themselves to oppress a Mind of any sensibility –'

At this point Mr Stott arrived again, no doubt to the relief of Michael Humble. The two men went out and that night Mr Humble prudently decided to avoid further confrontation. He stayed with the Duffields at Townhill instead of in Sarah's cottage, setting off for Shooters Hill early the following morning with his sister Margaret in the carriage, and young William beside them.

This had been Sarah's last chance to plead her husband's innocence. She reflected on Mr Humble's own character:

> He is certainly a man of very strong prejudices and very jealous of the Honor of his own Judgment – He is also miserably deficient in the power of retention, and tells all he knows, or even thinks, wch is injurious to his own family.

Suspicions that Michael Humble himself might have been behind their failure to have William's discharge from bankruptcy certificate signed were too awful to contemplate and Sarah dismissed them:

> But I am sure he has not intentionally retarded the certificate by his communications as duplicity of character is by no means his failing.

Anxious to be fair, she remembered all his kindnesses to them in the past, and recently, when young Sally had been ill at Bath:

> . . . for if she had been his own daughter she coud not have received more kind or more constant attention from him

and his lovely departed wife [Michael Humble's wife Harriett died in 1805]. His heart is good and his intentions upright.

Sarah sent this report on her conversation with Mr Humble to Daniel Whittaker, open for his persual, and for forwarding to William, who had finally embarked for New York. Daniel sent on the lengthy document, enclosing his own opinion on the matter. Sarah had written him, he said affectionately to his brother, 'a very interesting sensible kind letter, strongly pressing me to visit Bradford – don't let this raise your jealousy'.

Daniel had read Sarah's account of the encounter with Michael Humble with admiration, and saluted her persuasive charm:

> You will find that there has been a meeting of explanation with Mr Humble, and I am of opinion there are few more capable of working on his feelings than Mrs W. I understand she is on a visit to the House and I do hope her good sence [sic] and perseverance in coming to an explanation will be productive of good consequences –

However, Daniel was only too well aware, as were they all, of Mr Humble's stubborn and choleric temperament. 'Some tempers and dispositions', he wrote, 'are very loath to give up a point or own they are in error.'

In a welter of good wishes for his brother's speedy return, Daniel advised him not to stay in America on any 'speculative or uncertain matter'. He urged him to consider his health and keep his family constantly in his mind. Hard hearts are sometimes brought to be kind, he added, optimistically, and included, as any sensible businessman would, 'a price list, thinking it might be of service'.

During this period, Daniel Whittaker was a great source of strength and his office a great convenience to his brother William, who naturally suffered from not having a business address of his own. In Liverpool, Daniel acted as a post office and general *factotum*, sending on letters, putting in bills of acceptance to the correct quarters ('I duly received yours this morning inclosing 2 Bills of Acceptance value £600 – one of which £200 being close on due I have put into Hughes and the other shall be sent up in due time') and sending on mysterious packages:

A Truss coverd with a Mat under wch appears to be a Wooden Box arrd today by Waggon from London directed to you.

Stabbing in the Dark

New York, 1806

Having safely reached New York by the beginning of August 1806, William reported on his situation in happy ignorance ('No vessel has arrivd here that left Liv [Liverpool] after us except the Rhoda and Betsy, therefore I have no letters') of the drama being played out in England between his wife and Michael Humble.

No progress whatsoever had been made with the distillery – as he probably half suspected before he sailed. He wrote to Daniel by the 'Ship Horatio' on the 1st September:

> I wrote a few lines the 2nd August on my arrival with the ships Swift and Indian Hunter with inclosures for SW. The person I therein mentioned as expected from Cuba has arrived and I find that the works for the Distillery have remaind in status quo and that during the continuance of war there is no inducement to prosecute the plan.

Not only had the distillery scheme made no progress, but other people had taken over the agent's work he had formerly done in Charleston, which was scarcely surprising as he had been absent for nearly two years:

> the Commission business is now conducted by a young man formerly with Madans – a Spanish clerk and an old friend of mine Mr L who was offerd a share to prevent opposition – Things being so arrangd here there is no obligation, nor is there any inducement for me to proceed there.

173

The talk in New York was all of the possibility of peace between France and Britain:

We have strong reports of Peace and by the latest acct. from Barbadoes, a Frigate in 20 days from E [England] had arrived with news of Preliminaries having been actually signed – these reports have caused considerable emotion here but many people think such a circumstance impossible under the present posture of affairs – If it shoud be true it will give a great shock to the trade of this Country, and indeed to all Neutral Carriers or neutralizers of Enemies Property.

The trade to Havana is overdone as formerly and for one Com Merch [Commission Merchant] there are 3 or 4, and as their establishments are necessarily very expensive, except in a few circumstances they are scarcely exceeded by the profits.

It was not surprising that William's American friends found the idea of peace between Britain and France as unwelcome as it was astonishing. Much of their trade depended on the fact that the two superpowers remained at war, trying to block each other's trading routes. Neutral American ships were greatly in demand by desperate businessmen.

As 1806 advanced, Britain, France and America continued to issue orders and counter-orders to interfere with each other's sea trade. In November 1806, Napoleon issued his Berlin Decree which declared that, far from suffering a blockade by Britain, France would counter-blockade Britain instead. All commerce and correspondence between England and Europe was forbidden, all ships and goods were declared forfeit.

In return England issued Orders in Council forbidding neutral vessels to trade between ports closed to British ships, such as French ports and those of her allies. This restriction affected American trade, and friction between Britain and America remained high throughout this period. (Anger at

Britain's Orders in Council was to result in the passing by the American Congress of the Embargo Act of 1807 which closed American ports to all foreign ships, and the Non-Intercourse Act of 1808 which forbade trade with Britain. Four years later war broke out between Britain and America.)

Although the restrictive orders were certainly not helpful to business people, the prospect of peace was apparently even more disagreeable. William reported a few days later:

> There are so many long faces here at the rumours of peace which come from so many quarters that it is generally expected to have taken place – We have news to hand of Augst 6th Ld Lauderdale gone to Paris and Nantes that peace was actually signed at Paris 20th July with Russia and all points agreed with England – from Gibraltar 16th August that it had been signed at Madrid the 4th August . . . These reports cause great alarm here and put a stop to trade as if the Yellow fever grippd the city which thank God is not the case.

The consternation of the New Yorkers was premature. The successive rumours which reached New York referred to the peace negotiations undertaken between Napoleon Bonaparte and Charles James Fox, who had become the new Prime Minister after the death of Pitt early in 1806. Fox was known as a peacemaker, where Pitt had always remained stalwartly bellicose. Lord Lauderdale was sent as Fox's special emissary to do battle with Talleyrand, Napoleon's wily first minister, but by the autumn, peace negotiations had broken down.

The war between Britain and France went on, and although the long American faces presumably became more cheerful, the autumn brought the customary disasters for shipping. Hurricanes swept the eastern seaboard of the United States, damaging and sinking not only merchant shipping but also the British and French naval vessels in the area:

> The weather has been uncommon cool the weeks last

A West Indiaman in a hurricane, 1805.

past. The violent gales occurred on this coast about the 21st August and again the 2nd September have made terrible destruction among the shipping; beyond what was ever before experienced – many foundered and none escaped some damage –

Some of Jerome Bonaparte's squadron have got into the Chesapeake dismasted and others have been seen at sea that were wrecks – Mr Strachan's is thereabout and some of them have suffered considerably . . .

Safely on dry land, however, with all possibilities of doing business apparently having vanished, William was able to enjoy the plentiful and novel pleasures of American harvest time:

Peaches are now in perfection from 5 dollars according to quality – an abundance of Apples and Pears. I eat peaches like a Yankee hog and am getting fat with them . . .

When the letters finally did arrive from England, they seemed at first to contain only pleasant concern for his welfare and family news, which did nothing to ruffle him.

Mr Humble had sent him 'a very affectionate kind letter in which he advises my not engaging in any speculation or business which might interfere with my return to my family. I have assured him again and again that I will not.'

William read all the news of family and friends, and was sorry to hear that:

> Mrs D did not derive any benefit from Harrowgate. The Old Lad [Mr Duffield] is so fond of self that I suppose he forgot you in his eagerness and anxiety for number 1 – J B [Sarah's brother John Buck] is I hope by now enjoying himself knee deep in Ing fog – it will be quite a treat after the durance he has suffered in Courtly Town – I told you he would soon know more about Bills – it was a narrow escape – a fine run Thing –

But when he settled down, perhaps with a bowl of peaches to hand, to read Sarah's separate account of her confrontation with Michael Humble, his contentment was rudely interrupted. So incensed did he become that he sat down to dash off, in his graceful handwriting, ten pages of closely-written rebuttal. His pen flying over the pages sprinkled them so heavily with indignant underlinings, rhetorical questions and extravagant fury that Sarah must have once more wished she had not tried to intervene. Her well-meant efforts had only served to drive her husband distracted.

William Whittaker, enigmatic, shadowy, injudicious, ineffective and unsuccessful, leaps into life in these pages. He struck back with bitter sarcasm at the tormentor who was also his benefactor, his carefully-cultivated eighteenth century urbanity vanishing into a romantic rage. His resentment was was all the greater because Michael Humble must have harboured this grudge for years, in spite of his apparent friendship.

William was 'mortified' that Sarah had 'thought it necessary to run after' Michael Humble, to explain 'what he had predetermined not to understand'.

William had realised that the amiable attitude of many people, including Michael Humble, towards him on his return to England was dependent on the possibility that the London court case would give him a respectable windfall from the insurers. And all of them, including his creditors, had been disappointed, and altered their opinions accordingly.

When they had spoken at Bath, Mr Humble had even offered William a partnership – at the very time when he might have expected an apology for the affair of the drawn bill.

The rhetorical questions came thick and fast:

> Where, I ask, was his conviction then that I was a *premeditating Villain*? Where that *Active resentment* that has since appeard against me? Were they lulled to sleep by the Prospect of fingering a few thousands?

> At Liverpool I requested he woud do me the justice to look over these papers and accounts which I left with him – he promised he woud – we shook hands and parted – Did my request imply that I allowed his suspicions to be just? On the contrary, it expressed a wish that he woud see his error – but he *jesuitically* implies that in so doing I acknowledged myself *wrong* in the full sense that woud make him *right* in his suspicion.

William wrote on indignantly. Mr Humble's criticism of William's voyages, he declared, was based on total ignorance of the situation he had been faced with in 1796:

> I wish that Mr H woud confine himself to facts – he speaks to you of the trade from Charleston to Havana in 1796 as 'speculative and uncertain and well known to be so' – Now I shoud like to know where he got his information and this foreknowledge, for previous to that time *there had never been foreign trade to Cuba* (except

Negroes) and there was not time for any Vessel to have returned *even to Charleston* at the time the Bill was presented in Liverpool.

Michael Humble had incautiously told Daniel Whittaker earlier that he thought William's American passport, with which he could travel all over Cuba, would ensure that he would make a rapid fortune. William's scorn knew no bounds:

> At the *former period* there were *great profits* both on the Out and Home cargoes (there being no stock of goods and plenty of produce) and *less risk* than at present. For a long time trade has been overdone and now every article is as well known there as it is here. There are no risks now except that of going to a glutted market which risk did not exist in 96 – Sea Attaque and Capture are now and always were the only Risks, Smuggling being avoided – now a Credit is given, formerly it was an exchange of *Goods* for Cash and or Produce.

Mr Humble's knowledge of the present situation was as minimal as his monumental ignorance of the past, insisted the bitter and furious voice of experience. William had, after all, been there:

> I was in Havana from Dec 96 (from Jamaica to Charleston) when War was declared against England – I was there when it was agreed to open the Port – I saild from there immedly the Embargo was lifted and took the first Intelligence of the opening of the Port – The Vessel I was in was the *first* that arrived in the United States with the news and I was among the first to return to Havana, and therefore I know as much on this subject as Mr H.

Sarah could never control her conscientious impulse to tell William absolutely every word which passed between her friends and relatives on the subject of her husband. Naturally enough, the idea that people were talking behind his back infuriated the victim.

Mr Humble had apparently 'enlightened' Mr and Mrs Duffield, wrote William sarcastically, as to William's real character drawn from his 'villainous conduct':

> We have an instance of his *Zeal* in the close intimacy he formed at T [Townhill] last year, in spite of well known strong prejudices, in order to *gain attention* for his Stories.

Michael Humble had criticised William to Mr Spear, to Mr Todd and – it seemed more and more likely – also to Mr Tipping:

> I have no doubt he has taken pains to make known my *unprincipled conduct* towards Fraser and my shameful neglect of Madans business – you say he 'no longer blames me' – had he then any reason or ground to do so? With respect to Madans, is it necessary to communicate to him every particular of every transaction to gain his goodwill and avoid his misrepresentations and calumnies? It woud be the same as to put them into the Daily Advertizer.

It is to be hoped that Sarah kept this letter to herself, or at least showed it discreetly only to Daniel, William's steadfast champion. William raged on:

> It would be more becoming in Mr H. as Merchant and a Religious Man were he to give more time to his business and less to the Dissemination of his Calumnies – it woud be the appearance at least of *'Doing All Things More For the Glory of God'*. But perhaps Mr H thinks me fair game for his sport and amusement.

As William covered his last page, his sense of the cruel injustice of his own position almost overcame him. Mr Humble had even criticised him for going back to America when the prosecution of the distillery plan at Matanzas was uncertain.

Why did I go? Why did I not write? What a question to come from him who had used every, the *meanest of means* to deprive me of the good opinion of the few friends I had left of all your friends – from him who had been at so much pains *to drive me away* – The whole of Mr H's conduct towards me, since he found there was no prospect of receiving much from the Underwriters, consequently *No Partnership* neither shews the goodness of his heart nor the uprightness of his intentions. It woud have been more Manly to have declard himself openly instead of enjoining you to Secrecy and then – Stabbing in the Dark.

William thought long and painfully about his first difficult days in Charleston, and Michael Humble's infuriating assertions. He wrote down his memories in jotted notes and kept them. They were collected up with his papers. One note reads:

Mr H remarked that if I had remained at Charleston, I shoud have made a fortune long ago and paid off every old debt –

Remark – let me enquire into the possibilities – I arrivd at Charleston in Oct 95 when all produce was high particularly Cotton and Rice – I declined doing anything either for myself or the House of H and Co but what was approved – I remaind till March doing nothing (board at 10 Drs. p. weeks exclusive of Liquors, washing etc.) then accepted an invitation to Jamaica free of all expence but my passage back which was in June at which time Cotton continued high and I had no orders or the least encouragement to do anything – the Sickly Season was fast approaching, early in July therefore I made another trip to Jamaica and returned by way of Havana to Charleston in December, where as before, I remained in Charleston till March without any employ or the least encouragement to expect any –

What he remembered most vividly, apart from the danger of mortal illness, was the depression caused by his isolation and inactivity:

had I continued in Charleston the Summer months I might have escaped with my life but I should have run great risk of the Lunatic Asylum – I had sufficient caution on my first arrival on seeing one poor object the only remains of a young man who had arrived there about two months before me in a Vessel from Scotland.

now we are so comfortably settled

Bradford, 1806-1810

In November 1806, William Whittaker arrived back in England after his abortive transatlantic journey, and he and Sarah took stock of their situation. It appeared that the act relating to debtors which had caused such rejoicing among the relatives of bankrupts still did not allow William 'to take up any profitable trade without exciting the activity of his Enemies'. Unable to threaten him further, however, the creditors finally abandoned their long campaign against him.

Sarah sent back the £200 which Michael Humble had advanced her towards their expenses, and, bruised and emotionally drained by their misfortunes, the Whittakers settled down thankfully to a modest country life in their cottage on the Townhill estate. William was to try a little farming on Sarah's land – an occupation for which he was probably totally unsuited. However, most businessmen of those times took it for granted that domestic life involved keeping their own poultry, pigs, and cows for milk. If he followed suit, at least William could make a small contribution to their expenses.

No more was heard about the quarrel with Michael Humble until the following spring when Sarah thanked him for agreeing to become a trustee for the children. He had made it plain that his concern was limited to herself and her son and daughter. She wrote:

> I woud have receivd great pleasure from your kind assurances of continued freindship did they not seem to

imply that I must not now expect it to to extend to a quarter Equally interesting to me.

Once more, still indefatigable, she tried to justify William's actions, and repeated their claim that money to repay Michael Humble's bill had been left with Mr Fraser at Charleston:

> An 'if' in your last letter, concerning Mr Fraser's Shipment, wounded me sensibly, but my cooler Judgment persuaded me I mistook your meaning . . .

A state of truce seems to have existed between Sarah and Mr Humble for a few months. They probably both kept to their own opinions, but letter writing ceased.

On the 5th December 1807, however, William and Sarah were alarmed and flustered to receive a totally unexpected proposal. The surprising Mr Humble, who was essentially kind-hearted, suddenly offered William one more opportunity to earn money in America. Although it was a generous and flattering offer, implying as it did that he now recognised William's probity, the idea filled them with dread. The last thing William wanted to do was to face another arduous trip across the Atlantic. Mr Humble's offer was couched thus:

> I give you a few lines to ask if you would like to go to the Havana, as supercargo of a ship we intend sending there – thinking it may be doing better for your family than farming if agreeable to your Wife – you shoud have £500 certain and everything found you on the voyage – & if the voyage turned out profitable we wd give you £200 in addition making it in all £700 – if you decline going be so good as to send me an assessment of cargo you woud approve.

William and Sarah prevaricated desperately. In their very much reduced circumstances, they dared not hastily reject such an idea, nor would it be prudent to risk offending the capricious Mr Humble yet again. Sarah wrote anxiously to Daniel:

> I shd be indeed very unwilling now we are so comfortably settled for my Husband to be again tempted to take up anything like residence at Havana or to wait for future cargoes – Mr W says if he coud get his business finished before the hot season commences 700£ wd be a most acceptable acquisition and perhaps it might be augmented by a little traffic on his own account – He is writing to Mr Humble to desire further particulars & offering if necessary to go over to Liverpool to talk matters over with him – as we conclude Mr Humble means his ship to sail as soon as possible – he makes use of my pen as he is busy writing to Mr Humble and in arranging his ideas as to the list he requests of a cargo. You coud perhaps furnish some useful hints on this head.

Sarah kept a copy of the long-winded and fatally unenthusiastic reply to the offer which William sent to Mr Humble – or did she actually compose the letter herself? Certainly her own loathing of the whole idea was barely concealed:

> Sir, Your favor was received Saturday – you will excuse the little delay in answering it as . . . a proposal so important to myself and family required mature deliberation – my own inclinations would certainly not lead me again to (embark on any adventure) [crossed out] to a foreign country and a tropical climate, when I am comfortably settled with my family in a state of that tranquillity and employment most suited to my taste and in which we both find contentment and happiness – but I have long been anxious to increase our means of comfort as our young Folks get forward in years and encreased expenses must be lookd for – Your proposal wd I am sensible in many respects afford an eligible

opportunity of doing this – We conclude you mean the vessel to sail as soon as possible that the goods may be early in the market – but I wish to know whether it is your intention for me to *return in the same vessel*.

A swift turn around would suit him best, 'as attended with the least personal risque', wrote William with sublime tactlessness. But how long did Mr Humble mean him to stay? It all depended on the type of cargo:

In *simple* cargoes (such as flour, rice, Lumber, wine) the former mode may be adopted without difficulty or sacrifice – But if the cargo is *assorted*, consisting mainly of dry goods, plantation utensils etc an immediate sale and closing of accts seldom or never can be effected witht sacrificing some part of the Cargo and I believe there is not so bad a market as Havanna for disposing of any articles not *immedy* called for – For Instance, pans, rollers, &c for the plantations are articles that have always paid large profits, but can not be sold wholesale witht great sacrifice – it woud beside cause a great detention of the vessel to sell them to tolerable advantage.

William offered to come to Liverpool for a discussion if this was necessary, and enclosed a list of articles which appeared to him 'the most favorable for the Havanna market'. On cutlery he gave a specific hint:

Should you send out any Birmingham ware (which I don't particularly recommend) omit sending forks with the Knives not being used there . . .

Mr. Humble's reply was speedy and to the point. In short, he washed his hands finally of William Whittaker:

You appear to prefer making a sacrifice of my interest to remaining longer on the spot, and for wch reason *I do not think it safe to engage you in this expedition.*

After this unnerving incident, silence reigned over the scene in Bradford for a year – or at least, none of the letters written that year were preserved. The whole family remained together, content to lead as uneventful a life as possible. William and Sarah were now nearly fifty, and for twenty years their lives had been hard and often miserable. Now they lived together in comparative peace, if not in prosperity.

The following December, their daughter, young 'Sally' (Sarah), went to visit her paternal relatives in Knutsford, where her parents hoped to join her. Her mother wrote to 'My Dearest Sally' in her old cheerful and sunny vein, chattering about Bradford life as she used to do in the old days. There was now even time to think and write about fashion:

> The Package of Tippets arrived at Townhill last evening where Wm and I had been dining and whilst we were in the act of opening and examining the contents of the parcel Mr Chas and Henry Faber arrived to whom I communicated Miss White's enlarged commission for Pelisses – tis well I had given up having one as I felt so large an order to be an encroachment on his obliging wish to accommodate Miss White and me by cutting what we want *at prime cost* whch is neither very profitable nor convenient for a merchant –

Bradford people still never miss the possibility of a good bargain through their connections in the textile world. Their ancestors of 1808 had the same acute appreciation of wholesale opportunities – as did Jenny Buck's sisters a generation before in the 1760s. Henry Faber's knowledge of London fashions was also much appreciated:

> He was so good as to say you may choose your color – if you prefer either the Sarragossa Brown, light Drabs or Amaranthus color, a sort of crimsonish tint wch will be fashionable according to their London orders he will let you have it – You will find the piece of Brown muslin among your Cloaths where I remember packing it in the

great portmanteau but as it will not be enough for sleeves I have desired Mrs Flint to send me some whch I hope to receive by Wednesday.

Sally's friends were missing her, said her mother:

Margaret Mossman tells me she has sent you a long letter to wch she expects a long and speedy answer – a monstrous sheet has arrived for you this morning and a more moderate one from Fanny Irwin –

Sometimes the lengthy communications in which the girls indulged could prove costly, as Sarah pointed out tartly:

Your last letter was charged double from being clumsily folded and thick paper.

Sally also received some typical family grumbling over handwriting. Young William sent thanks for his sister's letter via his mother, but regretted that the deciphering of it 'sent him to the Kingdom of Puzzledom'. Sarah's letter flowed on:

I hope your Ham arrived safe and undiscovered by the Sale mice – or any other set of depredations. I long to hear how it cuts up – the very day after you left an invitation arrived at Townhill from Mrs Peck – they spent a morning there, and the master of the house showd them all his Lions great and small and Mrs Hustler's garden besides – a pineapple also arrived of most excellent flavour –

I was at Leeds the other day – Mr D. lent me his carriage. The day was charming and I accomplished many little shoppings both for myself and Mrs Duffield – among the rest I discharged yr debt to Mrs Plinth who has made up a very extravagant bill double what we expected – when I was at Leeds I luckily met with a single pair of Bellows such as your Aunt Martha wishes for, wch I shall not fail to bring –

We hope also to bring a little pig for Grandma – Peggy

was deliverd Wednesday of 14, three dead, the other 11
very stout and lively –

Young Sally had described the the circle of relatives at
Knutsford as amiable, and at Brook Cottage her aunt's
'domestic scene agreeable and harmonious'. Her mother was
naturally anxious to hear all the details:

> I long to see my two little nephews and know not how
> you will be able to take leave of your two little
> Nurselings – I expect a long letter soon with a very
> particular account of all our dear friends not forgetting
> the 'snug Cottage and all its delights' – where tis well
> you arrived with no bones broken after your mad poney
> scamper, on wch occasion it must be confessed you
> exhibited more courage than sagacity.

Sarah had thankfully reached an age when she was no
longer expected to mount a horse, and a generation later, she
echoes Mrs Traviss's disapproval in 1772 of the horse-riding
exploits of her daughter, the dashing Ann Faber.

She was not entirely immune from foolishness herself, as
her next letter to Sally makes plain. She is writing, she says,
because, 'having lamed my foot by walking to Mrs. Town
yesterday in a pair of new shoes I am obliged to keep house
today'.

The Whittakers' planned visit to Knutsford, after which
Sarah and young Sally were to stay at Salford with Mrs
Simpson of Hart Hill, while William travelled to Liverpool,
was beset by various obstacles. Caroline Duffield had fallen
ill, and the family was worried about her. Young William too
had been ill – visiting Sedbergh, he had succumbed to a 'cold
and Fever'. This news alarmed his mother almost enough to
send her in that direction – but fortunately she soon received
word that he had recovered.

Caroline was causing more anxiety, and could not be left
without female assistance:

> Two impediments to my accompanying your Father

are I hope removed – Nurse Seed has no long engagement to prevent her being here and Mrs. Nicholson will be at Townhill in Feby the beginning of the month.

William's farming obligations were being taken with the utmost gravity, and William's voice, trying to impress on his wife the importance of his activities, is plainly discernible.

. . . if the weather prove favorable your Father hopes to get some Seed into the ground, in which case he thinks we shall be able to leave home about the 10th but must return for similar employment by the 20th – the state of the weather has a material influence on the motions of a Farmer, and it is difficult to speak with certainty, but as winter is now seriously coming, I hope a week or two of hard weather will be succeeded by a little mild sunshine wch will enable him to complete his projected labours – Fanny is to calve towards the end of February and we must be at home at her accouchement –

The lack of a private carriage was a penance for Sarah, and she wrote in some exasperation:

Your Aunt Sharpe mentioned a coach wch comes within two miles of Knutsford is that the Sunday one? Is there none wch comes to Knutsford?

But Caroline grew weaker. In her next letter Sarah reported grave news:

Mrs Duffield continues much as when I last wrote. I see her frequently but she is so very weak that I dare not stay with her more than five minutes at a time – as she exerts herself beyond her strength that that she may not give her friends the pain of seeing how very ill she is and suffers for it afterwards.

These are awful and affecting times, my dear Sarah, of wch I should willingly have spared you the particulars, but I know you woud suffer more by absence and that such scenes improve while they wound the heart.

On the 8th February Sarah finally abandoned her plans to leave Townhill, and called Sally home. It was arranged that Miss White would call for Sally in her own carriage, and take her to Manchester, whence, instructed her mother:

> if no escort can be found you must take your chance of meeting civil company in the coach. I shall write to Miss White by the Defiance tomorrow along with yr Aunt Martha's pair of bellows, for wch for safety's sake I shall pay the carriage –

The only surviving few lines of Caroline Duffield's handwriting are kept in a deed box separate from the Whittaker papers. Her son John Buck wrote on this scrap of paper, 'my dear mother's dying letter – January 1810'. In Caroline's few sentences there is a little vignette of life at Townhill, showing her bathed in the sentimental and rosy light of family concern:

> Your sister read me a most charming paper last night in The Spectator Thurs Oct 18 no. 515. I am better my dear John than when you left me and never in all my life more completely happy – your kind and affectionate behaviour has endeared you to me more than ever, and your father's affectionate attention is constant and unwearied his attachment to you is equal to that of a real father.
> Your Sister Mrs W has been eating roast beef with yr Father and plum pudding – she puts off her Knutsford journey. I am sorry – I am much better. I am extremely weak but that I must expect . . .

Caroline died soon afterwards. Her going left a large gap in the Townhill household, and the 'affectionate, kind' atmosphere rapidly dissolved. Family tensions turned into resentment and then open warfare.

a coolness in my manner

John and Sophia, 1810-1816

Soon after the restraining influence of his mother was removed, John Buck frightened his sister by picking a prodigious quarrel by letter with his stepfather Francis Duffield. He sent a copy of it to Sarah, with his explanation:

> This great packet will astonish you, but Mr Duffield's conduct has been such that I thought myself justified in writing the enclosed letter to him. Let Mr W step across with it to Calverley [to the Fabers] – perhaps you had better make a fair copy properly stopped and large Lettered where it is deficient.

The quarrel had begun immediately after Caroline's death, as John haughtily explained in his letter to his stepfather:

> Sir, You say you have observed a coolness in my manner of late and you demand an explanation. You shall have it. Within the week in which my Mother was buried, you attempted to impose on me in the transaction related to the Coals, this plan you must certainly have revolved in your mind even when my Mother was lying on her deathbed – I saw through your professions but rather than come to an open rupture, I was willing to concede a losing bargain –

The presence of coal on one's estate was not to be taken lightly and somehow, it is clear, Francis Duffield had stolen a march on his stepson. As the machine age gathered impetus, landowners became acutely aware of the importance of coal and iron under their fields, and mineral rights were by now eagerly sought. Bradford's mineral riches included the Black Bed coal seam, followed by a seam of ironstone, and below that the more valuable sulphur-free Better Bed coal seam which was highly prized in the manufacture of iron. In 1788 a Wakefield ironmaster, John Sturges, had been the first to recognise the coal and iron industry potential in the Bradford area, and had established the Bowling Ironworks.

The Duffield family was later to be closely connected with the coal and iron industry in Bradford, and probably Francis Duffield had already grasped the idea of a new way to riches. John Buck, who lived in London and did not have his finger as closely on the local pulse, may have regretted signing away mineral rights to his stepfather.

Selling all the mineral rights to one's land was a mixed blessing, however. Extensive mining ruined the land for any other purpose. Sir Francis Lindley Wood, a neighbouring Bradford landowner, was wary when he came to sell some of his estate to Sturges in 1814. In common with other colliery owners, he had used his coal in a modest way, mostly for domestic purposes, and he was far from sure that he wanted his whole estate 'reduced in appearance to a wilderness' – which would be the result of the wholesale exploitation of its resources.

John Buck obviously also had dealings with John Sturges, and was keen to get all that was due to him from working on his land. In a later letter he told Sarah:

> Sturges and Co owe me some money for a bit of Iron Stone got under my fields – the Collier knows all the circumstances – I should be much obliged if Mr W would ask them for the money, some ten pounds.

John Buck had a further complaint against his stepfather:

> All that part of the country knows that you have lived at Townhill for many years at a Rent shamefully low – during my Mother's life my Sister forebore to raise the

rent that your evidence of temper should render her unhappy – that cause being removed I advised her to ask for an increase in rent – you recollect how you acted on that occasion for a few paltry pounds – you appealed to the best feelings of my Sister's heart and made the memory of my Mother assist you in driving a hard bargain. But I prevented my Sister being so worked upon and when this failed, you declared we had entered into a conspiracy for the sole end of disturbing your quiet – and now you ask why I am cool to you –

By now in full flow of indignation, John also accused Francis Duffield of having not only secretly tucked away the plan of Townhill, but of having fraudulently undermeasured it. He was convinced, he said, 'that covetousness had taken such a hold on your heart that for the sake of saving a shilling you would stoop to any measure of meanness'.

It would be a waste of time, he added, with a Parthian shot, to draw to his stepfather's attention the fact that 'your advanced age and your infirmities must soon bring you to a state where riches cannot help you'.

John had earlier agreed to sell Francis Duffield a farm, and now 'condescended' to calling in the £5,000 purchase price, as he was contemplating marriage and needed the money to buy a house. He ended his diatribe by requesting that any further communication between them should be through Mr Faber or the attorney.

Sarah, living on the Townhill estate herself, naturally received the full force of Mr Duffield's indignant response, and tried to act as a peacemaker. She wrote hastily to her brother to tell him that the older man was not only 'much chafed' by this quarrelsome missive, but hurt as well as angry.

John wrote again, almost as full of *hauteur* as before, but agreeing that if the £5,000 for the farm were paid, he would dismiss the whole matter from his mind, and shake his stepfather by the hand as if nothing had happened. There were to be absolutely no further financial transactions between them, and he expressed the hope to Sarah that 'no further cause of irritation arise between us; I desire that he may not write to me on this subject, as it would not be proper for me to receive from him any letter of an humiliating nature'.

Although easily finding the time and inclination to quarrel with his stepfather, John Buck was preoccupied not only by his demanding work as a barrister, but by his impending marriage to his 'fair one', Sophia Brigstocke. The money he demanded from Francis Duffield was needed to buy 'a cage for my Bird of Paradise. This wonderful creature', he told Sarah wryly, 'is one of the eight children of a Welsh gentleman of family and fortune, and the Almighty never formed a sweeter temper which he has pleased to clothe with beauty –'

The Brigstocke family home was at Blaenpark, Carmarthen, whence John wrote to his sister, 'having played the truant the greater part of the Circuit. The law goes on very badly – I cannot serve two masters.'

Now that John was setting up an establishment of his own, he claimed his personal possessions from Townhill. Sarah packed up several parcels to go to London 'by the Waggon'. John had forgotten nothing:

> If it is not too great a trouble I should wish to have a catalogue of the few remaining books at Townhill which are not Mr Duffield's. The small glass painting in my bedroom which was given to me by Mr Sharp I should also wish to be packed up in a box made for the purpose to preclude the possibility of it being broken.
>
> If I recollect rightly you informed me that my dear Mother had left a ring or something of that sort of jewellery which she desired might be given to my wife if ever I should happen to have one. Whatever it might be, I should wish to have it made into a small parcel and sent off by one of the coaches immediately as

195

probably it may want resetting – have I not Miss Edgeworth's tales? It may be packed with them as small parcels are not infrequently lost.

Maria Edgeworth wrote highly popular romantic stories set in Ireland, and probably the book as well as the jewellery was intended as a present for the lovely Sophia.

In May 1812, John and Sophia were married, and set off on their honeymoon to Malvern Wells. In a scribbled honeymoon note John explained:

> Malvern is superior to the general style of watering places. We have a private apartment as this place is an hotel and not kept upon the Harrogate plan. I do not find my pen runs glibly and therefore shall conclude by telling you that the fairness of the weather, the beauty of the place, and my little Wife make time pass very pleasantly.

Harrogate, the Yorkshire spa, was full of lodging houses clustered thickly round the Pump Room and the baths. Malvern was clearly a cut above it, in the eyes of the sophisticated London honeymooners.

Less than a year later, in April 1813, John wrote to his sister from London:

> Yesterday at 5.30 a.m. my dear Sophia introduced into the bustling world a little girl. I am particular as to the time in order that you may get your son who is said to be a great scholar to cast the nativity.

In the excitement of the event, John became euphoric and, never missing a chance to display his breadth of knowledge, jokily philosophical:

> The technical term 'as well as can be expected' does not express how well both the mother and child are. The nurse makes use of the expression 'charmingly'. There never was so great a beauty seen – everybody says so.

Perhaps you may doubt it, never mind, there will be sceptics who doubt the best founded facts – the good Bishop Berkeley doubted of the existence of a material world, but notwithstanding that, if he had struck his knuckle against a piece of Derbyshire Spar he would have cried out Oh! – and so would you if you were to see my Baby exclaim Oh! what a beauty.

The following year, Francis Duffield began to fail. When he heard of his stepfather's illness, John regretted their quarrels, and apologised for his 'harshness and irritability':

I am a good deal affected by the interest he takes in my welfare. I do not doubt he will have satisfaction on hearing that I am as happy as a quiet and peacable home, a wife of whom I am very fond, a first child that is promising and healthy, and constant employment can make me – and to all these add the present hopes of sometime rising to eminence in an honorable profession.

Mr Duffield died that summer, and when John Buck went to Doctors Commons (Doctors Commons was the office of the serjeants-at-law, who practised the civil law, including probate) to read his stepfather's will, he exploded again. To his fury, the ungrateful cuckoo in their nest had left not a penny to Sarah or her children, but everything to his unprepossessing nephew, Francis Vincent. John was disappointed and vexed beyond measure:

And I must say that the injustice which he has shown to you and your family is only equalled by his disgusting vanity in requiring the mooncalf to take the family name of Duffield – I never wish to think of him or his Caliban again – I cannot do so with temper.

The new Francis Duffield, heir to his uncle's estate, continued to live at Townhill as Sarah's tenant. He founded a family to which there is a monument in Bradford Cathedral. They became influential in the industrial life of the city, and were known as 'the Duffields of Duffield Hall, formerly Townhill House'. They continued to patronise the arts, and their name is mentioned as 'a leading family of musical taste' at the founding of the Bradford Philharmonic Society in 1831.

John and Sophia's life in London for the next two years was busy and eventful. His clients included such notables as Lady Sitwell, to whom he was introduced by Mrs Stovin of Doncaster. He 'stewed in court' all the summer of 1813 and eventually had to admit that exhaustion had overtaken him. The doctor said that country air and a complete relaxation of mind for two months were necessary, so Sophia set off for Wales and John followed her as soon as he could. He wrote to his sister:

> Sophia departed here last Monday week with her Baby. I prevailed on her to quit London for the Welsh mountains as she had been much reduced by an inflammatory sore throat that attacked my family. The young one has got safely through the small-pox and is very stout and well.

Brother and sister discussed further the furniture and books at Townhill which did not belong to the new tenant. John asked Sarah not to sell any of his books if she could give them house-room. They also exchanged notes on books they had enjoyed and borrowed from the 'Circulating Library'. He wanted her to have any furniture which officially belonged to him, including a 'Chest of Drawers' which she liked. Sarah could have it, said John:

> in return for a Ham of your own feeding – I never yet remembered to tell you the fate of the last – it was together with some other articles stolen from my Kitchen by a person who left in exchange a pottle of raspberries, you see the trick; if the thief had been met were not the raspberries ordered here?

Sarah's hams and tongues were popular with the London

household, though sometimes the curing of the hams was not entirely successful:

> Many thanks for the Ham you have bespoken – owing to the last not being sufficiently cured we were obliged to throw away the largest portion of each but what remains is very good –

On their return to London, Sophia returned to a constant theme. She wanted young Sally, Sarah's daughter, to come and stay with her for a few weeks or months – for company, and probably to help look after the baby. John's patience was sorely tried, as he explained when he finally put pen to paper:

> My dear Sister, I have led the life of a dog for the past eight weeks purely on your account – it happens that I have married into what is called a very affectionate family – they feel it necessary to be vastly interested in each other's welfare – for instance when Robt Brigstocke was serving in the *Java*, and the news came of the capture of that ship without giving any particulars, my spouse saw that it was expedient for her to be vastly alarmed, and being near her time, the consequences were rather dangerous – I could forgive all this provided that she would let me and my Family be quiet – for the past eight weeks the daily salutation has been 'Well, have you written to your Sister yet?'

The Bucks seemed to enjoy the company of their young relatives, and both of them hospitably issued repeated invitations for young William and Sally to visit them. William was by now a student at St Johns College, Cambridge, and when he had taken his degree, said his uncle, he was to visit them to relax 'and ramble about as much as he pleases . . . His aunt is very anxious to see him as she wants to give him a lecture upon the arts, or to speak more exactly on the tying of a neckcloth, for she says her late master Mr Ketch has taught her to tye it very roguishly.'

News of the baby was good, although the proud father's grasp of the normal progress of a mother and baby seems astonishingly feeble:

> The little child and its mother are both very well, and Sophia has not been since her confinement so stout as she formerly was – the young one's name is Caroline called so after my dear Mother and one of her aunts – The young one has got her legs, which came some time since, but her teeth are not yet arrived.

The following September, 1814, Sophia's second child was born at Ryde on the Isle of Wight, as a great fireworks exhibition took place in the park – perhaps celebrating the defeat of Napoleon and the imminent peace-making Congress of Vienna, or possibly the centenary of the House of Hanover.

John Buck was as euphoric as he had been on the birth of his daughter Caroline – and even more prone to literary flights. If Bishop Berkeley had inspired him on his daughter's birth, it was the distinctive style of Laurence Sterne, the fanciful cleric and author of *Tristram Shandy*, which John Buck borrowed on the birth of his son – 'paternal nonsense', as he described it later:

> My dear Sister, I make all haste to acquaint you that my Spouse has made me a present of a little Boy – Poor Sophia had a bad time of it. She was in labour from Friday till the Monday night following – I thought we should have lost the young one – he had taken very ill with I believe the measles within a few days of being born, which I am informed is customary when the mother has had that disorder during her term of her pregnancy. The lad and his mother are now both of them doing well – I have christened him John, though I am not clear that in doing so I have acted properly – for he was born in the very instant of the great firework exhibition in the Park –
>
> Surely, I said in the Shandean style, he shall be

christened and called by a name that shall commem-
morate the fortunate moment when he was born – the
name emblematical of that rising salient principle by
which his life is to be characterized. Rocket he shall be
called. But afterwards recollecting that however brilliant
its course may be, a Rocket always tumbles at last and
ends in a stick, I determined to stick by the old name,
and John he is called, much at your service.

Unfortunately, in the bleak January of 1815, little John
fell seriously ill, perhaps already weakened by his bout of
measles:

> I received your letter on Saturday, when our little Boy
> was attacked with the Croup, or something like it, in his
> throat. The immediate application of Leeches prevented
> instant death, but the effect of the disease threw him
> into convulsions for nearly eight and forty hours – on
> Friday he was pronounceed out of danger, but the
> complaint has returned, they are applying blisters to his
> throat but I am afraid without much hope of success –

The household was in a turmoil. Sophia, who had herself
been ailing, was 'nearly harassed to death', and the baby's
nurse had to be dismissed for bad conduct. John was
frantically busy in chambers, inundated with more work than
ever before. He finished his catalogue of disaster wearily:

> On reading my letter, I can hardly make sense of it,
> but I am too much fagged to write another.

Three weeks later, after a prolonged struggle, the baby
died. Although parents in that era were inured to the deaths
of infants, their anguish was no less acute than it would be
today. John sent his sister a heartrending account of the
trauma:

> Our little boy died on Sunday night a month after his
> first attack – I really now feel as if a load was taken
> from off my heart – For the pain he suffered and the

201

noise he made owing to the compression of his throat
was dreadful to see and hear – It was impossible to be
in any part of the house and not hear him. Another
fortnight would have destroyed his mother. As it is she
is much reduced, but I hope by sending her to some
friends of ours who live about ten miles from Town that
all serious consequences may be prevented, as Country
air and changing the scene will tend to restore her in
body and mind.

In his distress, John blamed the doctor for not understanding the illness, and ordered a post mortem on the baby:

> I resolved to have him opened, which was done last
> night. I have not yet seen the gentleman who performed
> the operation but the Nurse tells me that it appears he
> died of an inflammation of the Heart that had extended
> from the throat where it commenced – the inflammation
> in the throat being what is technically called the Chronic
> Cough – I shall have the particulars more accurately
> from the operator when I see him –

Sarah had done her best to help, sending advice and
remedies which she had successfully used with her own
daughter:

> We tried the remedies that were successful with Sarah
> – you have got great credit for your description of the
> Complaint it is said to be as accurate as though drawn
> up by a Medical Man.

Poor little John arrived amid rejoicing, and was indeed
snuffed out just like the rockets which marked his birth four
months earlier.

Two months after the baby's death, John was writing from
'Surry' where he and his family were spending their Easter
holidays. Sophia had recovered to some extent, and was
concentrating on her little daughter. The letter is laboriously

headed with some Roman numerals – 'March XXVII
MMDCCCXIII':

My dear Sister, We think our little girl very
accomplished and her Mama desires you to believe that
she executed the date of this letter with her little fingers.
Whether she did or not I shall not take it upon myself
to declare, but there is supposed to be something very
mysterious in it and it is supposed to relate to
Bonaparte.

It certainly was mysterious, as the date should have read
the 27th March 1815, not 2813. It was a fateful year, and a
month which sent a shiver of alarm through Europe.
Napoleon Bonaparte had been defeated and banished to the
island of Elba. But within two months of arriving in his island
exile, he had escaped and was back on the French mainland
gathering yet another army. This was the beginning of the
'Hundred Days' of Napoleon's last campaign, which was to
end on the field of Waterloo.

Sarah had obviously been an admirer of the dynamic
French emperor, perhaps because his forceful style was so
much in contrast to that of her gentle and ineffectual
husband. Her brother could not resist a caustic dig at her
wrong-headed foolishness, with an apt description taken from
Gray's poem *The Bard*:

I congratulate you on the return of Bonaparte,
especially if you have increased your expenses on the
strength of the peace establishment – Do not Gray's
lines apply quite pat to this great man – 'amazement in
his van with flight combined and sorrow's faded form
and income tax behind'.

It was of course solitude which followed Edward III in the
poem, not income tax. But income tax to the wealthy Buck
family was a topical point worthy of John Buck's satire, and
an imposition which they had suffered throughout the

Napoleonic Wars. By 1814 it soared to unprecedented heights, and now, when they had thought the war was finally over, they could expect it to rise again if hostilities were resumed against the French.

Money matters were very much John Buck's province. He was a lawyer, a wealthy landowner, and fully versed in all the problems of investment and prudent disposal of assets. He advised the family on all their financial affairs.

On his marriage, he gave his nephew young William all his rents for a certain part of his farm property, on the understanding that the interest of £120 per annum was to be paid to Sarah during her lifetime. He steered the family through the legal niceties of this gift to ensure its safety. He also set up an income for his niece young Sally, who was to pay her own income tax. He advised authoritatively:

> I think Sarah's money ought to be laid out in the funds, the 3 per cents, being now at sixty-five and a small fraction . . . William, like all other purchasers must pay for his conveyance − If the real estate be converted into Money, William must recollect to make his Will, for his Father's creditors should he die intestate will become entitled to it.

The arrangements for the payment of the incomes of Sarah and her daughter seem laborious, but, according to the custom of the time, only the men handled serious money. The women's funds were put in the names of Henry Faber and young William. The women were to sign a deed which would enable John Buck to collect the dividends on their behalf in London. It would be simple then for the invaluable Henry Faber to bring the money regularly for both Sarah and Sally, using the cash he collected for John's Bradford rents. In April 1815, when these arrangements were in effect, John noted that Sarah's dividend was £50 12s 6d and Sally's £4 2s 8d.

Sarah, conscious that she and William were fast approaching old age, consulted John about their own financial situation. In 1813 they decided to purchase a joint annuity. John suggested they buy it the following July, his words having a decidedly familiar ring, exactly like a present-day pension adviser:

> By doing so you will in the meantime receive a year's income at the old Rate – and the year's payment of the Government annuity will become payable the 10th of October following – Your lives must be ascertained by verification of the registrar of Births and Baptism, or if the register cannot be procured, by certain forms required by the Act – I will send you a set of printed forms and a Table of the rates that you may be prepared with all the requisites.

William Whittaker may have been dismayed at the way his brother-in-law authoritatively assumed command of their finances – but he was in no position to object. Not only did John Buck advise, but he had also provided for young William and Sally, as well as for his sister, something their father was humiliatingly unable to do.

Later that year John reminded the Whittakers yet again that young William must remember to make his will. If he did not, on his death, all the money which his uncle had allocated to him would vanish into the hands of his father's creditors. Even as late as this in his life, William Whittaker was haunted by his business failure of so long ago, and the reminders from his brother-in-law must have rubbed salt into the old wound.

John Buck was also interested at this time in the possible sale of some of his land – the first indication that one of his farms might be worth more as building land than for letting to a tenant farmer. The industrial advance of Bradford was becoming more and more rapid, and intense pressure was building up for land like that of the Bucks, so near to the centre of the developing town:

> Sadler Green wishes to make a deal with me for some

building land in the back lane. He offered half the
ground rent of a former place I let to him, and proposed
to lay the Fields out with a street through the middle of
it and a row of houses facing the back lane – I shall be
much obliged by Mr W. giving me his Ideas on this
subject and I should also wish to know if there is, in
the Iron Chest, a plan of the farm. I would not go to any
great expence, as accuracy of measurement is not what
I require –

Later in the same year, he was still thinking about it and
asking his brother-in-law's opinion:

I have some thoughts of putting my farm up to auction
– I understand the Bradford people are now so rich they
will buy at any price. Tell me what Mr W thinks on the
subject –

As 1815 advanced, Sarah found herself in indifferent
health. She suffered from knee trouble and found difficulty
in walking. But she finally allowed her daughter to visit the
Bucks in London and she arrived, escorted by her brother,
at 31 Montague Place, the Bucks' town house.

A few days later, both Sophia and Sally sat down together
to write to Sarah in Bradford – the only letters extant from
either of them. Sally wrote her letter below her aunt's to save
paper and postage. Sophia began, rather formally:

Believe me, my dear Madam, I feel fully sensible of
your kindness in allowing your Daughter to leave home
at a time when you could so little spare her. I assure
you I was most agreeably surprised by her unexpected
arrival, and trust that I shall be able to make her
comfortable and happy. She is already a great favourite
of my little darling.

Sally's letter also began solicitously, if a shade guiltily.

She had been out to buy some foolscap to write her letters and promised 'a few journals', which she hoped would not be too 'silly'. She hoped to hear soon 'how you and my Father bear my absence. Pray take care of your poor knee and recollect that when you limp, "you and I and all of us fall down"'.

Her impressions of the Buck family were duly recorded. Sophia, it was noticeable, enjoyed the company of her handsome young nephew, and poor Sally felt she could scarcely compete with her brother:

> Little Caroline is a sweet child – we shall soon be very thick. My Uncle looks better now than when we first arrived, he is thinner than formerly. I suppose Mrs Buck has told you all about herself. She is very pretty – less than I am, neither fat nor thin, her manners are very pleasant. She has never called me anything but 'Sarah'. I'm sure you would be fond of her. I wish she liked me as well as she does Wm. but am afraid that she will not.

Sophia thanked Sarah for sending a miniature of her husband, 'It is certainly like your brother, but not looking so good-tempered, the lower part of the face I think like my little Caroline'.

Sally also told her mother about an interesting call she had made with her aunt:

> We have been calling at Mrs Nairne's this morning – she desired I would tell you that she was mending a Tablecloth which belonged to the Prince of Wales our King's father. [George III's father died when Prince of Wales]

Sophia told Sarah about the treats she had planned for her young guests. It was not surprising that the young Whittakers enjoyed visiting their London relatives, with their fashionable household and easy, sophisticated manners:

207

I was glad to see William looking better than he did last year, he is going to Drury Lane this evening to see Kean in Richard the Third and I am in hopes we shall succeed in getting a Box tomorrow to see Miss O'Neil in The Grecian Daughter. [*The Grecian Daughter*, a play by Arthur Murphy, 1772]

scarcely a fit place for any Christian to live

Leaving Bradford, 1815-1820

Sarah and William Whittaker stayed at home during 1815. William was forced to wrestle with one more series of letters accusing him of wrong doing in 1795, the year he had first sailed for America. Thomas Boardman, a creditor of Sarah's uncle Stephen Todd's estate, began to pursue William actively for £500 which had been lent for his flight to Charleston. William shuffled his papers wearily. He had inadequate records of this loan, and Thomas Boardman seemed to be accusing him of having spent two amounts of £500, not one.

William was becoming tired and old, and it was too much trouble to justify his actions yet again. He wrote drafts of letters, full of crossings out and garbled explanations. Sarah helped as best she could. To their assistance came their old Lancaster friend Ben Satterthwaite, who had supported his friends during their ordeal by bankruptcy. He acted as their intermediary, trying to explain William's side of the affair. Mr Boardman probably never got his money.

At the end of 1815, John Buck commiserated with his sister on her 'home being quite a hospital'. William Whittaker fell seriously ill, was 'forbid exercise' and could no longer act as John Buck's Denholme rent collector. There is a gap in the letter-writing, understandable in the circumstances.

William died on the 16th June 1816, and all that records his passing is a lengthy and lugubrious funeral account rendered to Mrs Whittaker a month later. The sombre splendour of his funeral was Sarah's last touching attempt to accord her beloved husband the respect and dignity which he had failed to achieve during his lifetime.

Jonas Ingham's account, on a letterhead decorated with a hearse and funeral coach mounting a hill towards the church, detailed the cost of black crêpe, bombazine, a silk handkerchief, shawl, black cotton hose, ribbons, double twill 'sarsnett', white kid gloves, a mourning coach and hearse with horses for each vehicle, horse cloths, pall, trimming for the mutes' staffs, eleven black cloaks and top coats. Cash was paid to mutes, bearers and drivers, duty was paid, and fees to the vicar and 'saxton'. The funeral cost £28 5s 4d. On the back of this bill, Sarah added up her other expenses, which included £22 for mourning rings, £14 for the surgeon, and five guineas for Dr Mossman.

After William's funeral, Sarah disappears from view for some time. During this period, however, she made up her mind to leave Bradford, and departed with her daughter Sally to live at Toxteth Park, Liverpool. They rented a house in what was at this time a favoured and pleasant residential area. Young William became a Fellow of St Johns College, Cambridge, and decided to enter the Church.

His old friend and schoolmaster, the Reverend James Barmby, also left Bradford, having become a vicar at Melsonby near Richmond. In 1820 he wrote to his former pupil, young William Whittaker, at Cambridge, and it is from him that we can deduce the feelings of the old Bradfordians to the developments in the town. Mr. Barmby, a son-in-law of the Pollard family of Scarr Hill, frequently visited his relatives in Bradford. He wrote:

I have just returned from a visit to Scarr H [Hill] – The dirt and smoke of Bradford struck me exceedingly, coming from the pure air of the country. I remarked that your Mother and myself had quitted our residence at Bradford at the right time, as the town is becoming every day less and less agreeable and is really now scarcely a fit place for any Christian to live.

Mr Barmby's opinion was shared by many. The rapid rise of Bradford's industry had continued, unchecked by the depression which for many followed the end of the Napoleonic Wars. In 1821 the population had risen to over 26,000, and there were twenty worsted spinning mills. There was a major 'smoke nuisance', and the pell-mell development had proceeded without any regard to planning. As well as the textile mills, there was coal and ironstone mining and extensive quarrying. The Bradford beck was dangerously polluted and disease was rife.

Although old Bradfordians might shake their heads sadly, fortunes had been made with amazing speed, and men who had started at the looms had risen to own mills and handsome houses. Propertied local people, who had lived for generations surrounded by peaceful fields, found their land suddenly rocketing in price. The tradition of finding a good tenant for one's house, farm or fields was rudely upset. People began to think more of the possibility of a huge capital gain by selling for development.

Bradford in 1835.

211

In 1820, Sarah came back to Bradford, accompanied by Margaret Humble, to take advice from Mr Humble and her local friends about the future of Townhill and her land. It was winter – and the snow so deep in Halifax, she noted, that two horses had been lost in it. She stayed in her old house on the estate, in which she sat to write to her daughter Sally. She headed the letter with a French revolutionary flourish – 'Ci-Devant Drawing Room Wednesday morning' – and described their journey from Liverpool with her usual sparkle:

> My dearest Salakin, Here we are safe and sound after a very prosperous Journey we had 2 Gentlemen in the Coach who possessed those two valuable requisites in travelling companions – silence and civility, although these were counterbalanced by enormous great Coats and well crammed pockets and a very dirty Pillow on wch after offering both to Margaret and I they reposed all the day – and when Daylight came we were glad we had declined the offered down for I have seldom seen what shd be white so completely the reverse – we reached the Swan at the usual hour and according to yr direction I found Margaret waiting and I was heartily glad to recognise her old Pelisse – my Cousin Dawson was also in attendance –

The other Margaret who was waiting for the two ladies was young Sally's friend Margaret Mossman, the daughter of the celebrated and much-loved Bradford physician, Doctor Mossman, who lived in Hall Ings. He was, according to the nineteenth century journalist William Cudworth, 'the beau ideal of English gentlemen, tall, handsome and witty, life and soul of the circle in which he lived'. Sadly, he died insolvent.

Margaret Mossman acted as companion to another well-known Bradford figure, Miss Swaine, who lived in Chapel Lane. Margaret Mossman was in a state of great excitement as she met the coach, for it had been proposed that she

should escape from her attendance on the ailing Miss Swaine
and accompany Sarah back to Liverpool for a holiday. Sarah
noted Margaret Mossman's nervous state with her usual
sensitivity:

> Peggy stopped a few minutes with Miss Swaine – it
> is quite a settled business (as far as human affairs are
> ever settled) that she goes back with me. I think Miss
> Swaine is very poorly but she is so happy with
> anticipating the pleasure that Margaret will feel that she
> does not at all suffer herself to feel her own loss –
> Margaret is almost in trembling for the Journey lest
> something shd happen to prevent it – She walkd up with
> me that I might look in my Trunk for your Packet wch
> she ran off with immediately –

It was understood, Miss Swaine told Sarah, 'that the Doctor
is highly delighted and proud of the invitation and so anxious
his daughter shd accept as if displeased with her reluctance
to decide – and he has told her he will do *something
handsome*, but has not said what, and perhaps will not until
the very last.'

Doctor Mossman had his reputation for generosity to keep
up but, amusingly, was vague as to the details. Sarah,
meanwhile, reported on her relatives and friends – and the
cat:

> I am sorry to say I found my cousin Dawson [Humble]
> very poorly in his old complaint, and his other old
> complaint (dislike to medical aid) is also too strong to
> let Mr Sharpe be sent for – Mrs Humble has a cough for
> wch I am going to get her the material for the Toulic
> Medicine. The day before I arrived Titmouse got her
> Bed and produced 5 Kittens 2 of wch were so like her
> they were preserved. She sat on my knee at tea-time and
> purrd so contentedly that I coud almost fancy she knew
> me – I have a letter this morning from Mrs Fielden
> urging me to take Didsbury and Sale in on my way home

– She wd meet me in Manchester and take me to
Didsbury and the next day to Sale whence I could
proceed by the boat by way of Runcorn to Liverpool –

Mrs Fielden of Didsbury was to become young William's
future mother-in-law. Her proposal was an intriguing one,
and Sarah was tempted. The idea of sailing from Sale to
Liverpool on the canal was a delightfully different prospect
from the trundling coach.

'If I hadn't had Margaret with me I think I shd have done
it', declared the adventurous Mrs Whittaker.

The excellent old vicar Mr Thomas Faber was still thriving
at a very advanced age for his time. (He died in 1821, aged
ninety-one.) Sarah reported that:

George Pollard called a while ago at Calverley and
found Mr Faber's housekeeper toasting him his fourth
muffin – poor Tetley has had to pay £14 for selling our
wine. I must make him a handsome present. The penalty
was mitigated or it might have been £50. This house is
not yet let –

'Tetley' appears to have fallen foul of the excise laws in
selling off the Whittakers' wine cellar on Sarah's behalf.

The most important conversation during this visit was with
Michael Humble. He strongly advised her to sell Townhill,
and thought it was lucky Mr Duffield had not accepted
Sarah's offer to sell the previous year. He had had a great
deal of talk, he told her, with 'a Gentleman who would like
to purchase it if Mr Duffield did not'.

After this advice, Sarah seriously considered giving the
Duffields notice to quit Townhill, but with typical Bradford
caution, hesitated:

I have returned the Townhill call, and waved [waived]
for a few weeks giving my ultimatum – you see how
diplomatique I have grown.

Selling the land was a different matter, said Mr Humble:

214

He wd not by any means sell the lower half of the Ing
and adjacent Feilds − as this new road will sometime
and perhaps shortly bring them into streets and for the
limited quantity he would not take less than £6000. He
advises to have it put up for auction and buy it in if not
bid for to its full value.

Sarah was also being asked to exchange some of her land
at Penny Oaks with a Mr Wrighton, a plan which 'the new
road' to Leeds would make advantageous to both of them. In
her next letter, however, she reported that she had rejected
this offer.

Sarah was worried about young Sally's health:

I am sorry to find your foot continues to heat after
exercise I wish you woud contrive to make a linnen
Stocking laced as Mr Worthington described and send
for him if it at all encreases. I do desire and command
that you go not on either Sunday or Monday to the
Harrington School or Bible visiting.

While poor Sally was hobbling miles to perform good
works, her mother was engaged in less arduous outings, and
no doubt enjoying sharing the cost of hiring a carriage with
Margaret Humble:

I ordered a chaise early last Monday morning which
took us first to see Mr Humble's cottage at Idle whch
will be a very comfortable home and a charming summer
situation.

The new house at Idle was later named Quarry Cottage.
From there the two ladies drove on across the Bradford hills,
making the most of their day out:

Thence we proceeded to Calverley, found Mrs Faber
was rode out − then we went to call on Mrs North at
Wrose − from Wrose to Scarr Hill and from Scarr Hill
to Crow Trees − where we had a snug day only ourselves
and Mrs Pollard senior, Mrs W Pollard better in spirits

215

than when we were last there but not her former self,
she has 2 sweet children, 1 the Baby the most engaging
little creature I ever saw –

Sarah and Margaret Humble were also invited to dinner by
Mr Dawson of Royds Hall. He was kind enough to send a
carriage for them, but Sarah was not impressed:

> Mr Dawson's carr both took us and conveyd us home
> and a complete Jolting Match it was. Tomorrow we are
> to spend the afternoon and evening at Dr Mossman's,
> the first invitation I believe he has ever given to Ladies.

Shopping for the Liverpool house also occupied Sarah and
Margaret Humble:

> I have got drugget for the Drawing Room at 3/6 a yard
> the same color as the Parlour, but so much better quality
> that by order of my oracle Margaret I ordered enough
> for the whole room and then Wm may parade as he
> pleases – let there be a fire in Margaret's [Mossman]
> room on Monday –

On her return to Liverpool, Sarah began to think very
seriously about the future. She wanted her daughter Sally to
share equally with her brother in the assets she would leave
them. It was perhaps clear that Sally was unlikely to marry
as she was already nearly thirty.

Sarah consulted her brother John Buck about making her
will. His reply was detailed and contained much excellent
advice. He also warned her against too precipitate a decision
on selling her property. He agreed with her decision to make
an equal division of her assets between her two children, but
advised her, in the customary fashion, to leave the estate to
her son, charging him with paying his sister's 'fortune'.

William would have to pay out more than half the money
from rents in order to give his sister an income equal to the
investment income she would have had on the capital. In
return, if Sarah's will did not 'fetter him', he would have the

freedom to dispose of the estate at the most advantageous time. Because William's income as a clergyman would not survive him, young Sarah's fortune might be secured to William's children in case she died without leaving any of her own.

Sarah was to locate a copy of her marriage settlement so that John could check what power she had to dispose of her property as she wished:

> I think it would be better for your will to be drawn by a good conveyancer here in London than by a country atty [attorney]. It may cost you perhaps a guinea or two more but then again it may save you many a guinea being expended in law. Send me a copy of the settlement which I think H. Faber or Hailstone has, and say how much you intend for Sarah, and I will get everything done for you.

Thus, roundly disposing of provincial solicitors and asking to review the sensible provisions made so many years before on Sarah's marriage, John Buck prepared to draw up his sister's will. It was the last letter he sent her, and she wrote on it, 'my dear and ever lamented Brother's last letter to me about my will'.

John William Buck, barrister, and expert in the law of bankruptcy, on which subject he wrote a number of important cases for the law reports, died in 1821 at the early age of forty-one.

more like a Rabbit Warren than part of a Town

The Last Chapter, 1822-1837

In 1822 young William was appointed as Vicar of Blackburn, and, now that his salad days were over, settled down to become a solemn and reverend gentleman. His mother and sister, intensely proud of his Good Friday sermon in the *Blackburn Mail*, showed it to the pious Humble relatives, who were suitably impressed by his 'edifying' words.

In the only letter which survives from the Reverend William Whittaker, he gives intriguing sidelights on religious affairs – and his own attitudes. He found it an event worth remarking that 'Rebecca Sturges last Sunday *preached* in the Methodist Chapel at Doncaster'. Although the idea of a female preacher clearly shocked the young clergyman, radical ideas were expected from the Methodists. Far more deplorable was an incident in a neighbouring church after his friend the vicar had departed on his honeymoon, leaving the curate in charge:

> The little curate, Solomon Howarth, praught [preached] a sermon wch gave general offence. If I recollect aright, his text was: 'thou hast granted him his heart's desire and hast not denied the desire of his *lips*.'

> He talked about Adam and Eve, all *naked*, in the paradise of matrimony, about Samson and Delilah, David and Bathsheba and God knows how many others recorded in Scripture. In indecency he quite out-Heroded Wm Atkinson. No lady could hold her head up, and many left the Church. He has been chasseed

218

out of bonny Bradford, and is now curate at Richmond, but what share this offence had in causing his dismissal I cannot ascertain. The Vicar is extremely indignant, and is in a furious passion. So is his lady.

Priggish though he sounds, William was soon to find his own 'heart's desire' granted, in the shape of Mary Fielden. Sarah, match-making furiously, probably in conjunction with Mrs Fielden of Didsbury, invited Miss Fielden to stay during one of William's visits, and forewarned him with a typically light touch:

> I think a change of air, particularly Park air might be beneficial to her and if she happens to be here at the same time as your return from Bradford, I suspect neither party would think it more a propos.

William and Mary were to marry in 1825 and had nine children. Sarah and her daughter continued to live at Toxteth Park until the autumn of 1823, when they moved to Castle Hill, Lancaster. None of the Bradford land had yet been sold, and the Duffields were still the tenants of Townhill.

It was difficult to find a knowledgeable property professional to advise them on the disposal of the Bradford estate. Sarah had discovered from Stephen Humble, her cousin Dawson's son, that some fields near her own had been sold for six shillings a yard. Stephen would probably agree to act as her agent, but Sarah did not favour this. They needed somebody 'sufficiently Judicious and trustworthy to be our agent who has the necessary experience and is free from any other interests'. Stephen apparently did not fulfil these requirements.

Stephen Humble, with his wife Sarah and Stephen's parents, now lived at Quarry Cottage, Idle, Michael Humble having sold his Yorkshire properties and retired to Liverpool. (Quarry Cottage, later renamed Briarfield, became celebrated as the home of the pious and benevolent Mrs Humble, who founded the Unitarian church in the village of Idle.)

219

In 1825 young Doctor John Simpson, a Bradford physician, commented in his diary on the rocketing land prices in Bradford when he wanted to find some land to build a dispensary. It was by then impossible to purchase land adjoining the town by the acre – it had to be by the yard, and the price varied with the situation. Between 1820 and 1825, the price of land in the centre of the town had shot up from five shillings a yard to one guinea, or even up to three guineas.

Sarah sent her son a plan of the Townhill estate before the house was built, and explained:

> when the road was opened for a Street below the old House and the wall which ran the length of our two Feilds, we engaged to give 2 yards all the way down to Boggart lane as soon as it may be required.

This had been a mistake, as it turned out – grand gestures of the old days in giving precious yards were now being regretted. But Sarah was even more thoughtful about the consequences of selling her fields to an unscrupulous developer. She disapproved strongly of the chaotic development which was going on in Bradford, examples of which were already in place at the lower end of her estate. In fact she was appalled at the despoliation wrought by unchecked industrialisation, and longed for some sensible planning authority.

It was especially noticeable that while the church prepared to erect magnificent new places of worship, inadequate dwelling houses for the mill-workers were being thrown up in a jumble of crowded streets. She wrote:

> There are two new Churches going to be built in Bradford parish, one at Shipley and another at Wilsden and I see by the paper that an architect from Halifax is employed – I fear that the scientific improvements at Bradford do not extend to architecture – indeed I expect

220

the kind of buildings most in request are of the lower order, or such as Mrs Reed's.

But shd any be built on our land I wd wish some rule as to the Symetry to be fixd on, that any new Streets may not be in such hurried style and disagreement as to height and projection such as disgraces the erections between the Old House and Dead Lane –

When William went to Bradford, wrote his mother, he would be struck by the changes since he had last visited it:

You will I fancy call at Townhill and be struck by many alterations both of persons and our old premises and the Feilds in which your poor father used to delight

The following spring, in 1824, Sarah made a further determined attempt to come to a decision. She and her daughter Sally visited Blackburn Vicarage and then set off for Bradford by coach. They stayed the night at the Talbot, and then had 'a pleasant journey through a pleasant country – the new road from Keighley to Bradford is delightful'.

Then they arrived at their lodgings in Mrs Reed's house at the lower end of the Townhill estate, visited Miss Swaine, who scarcely recognised them, and then Townhill, where the younger Mr Duffield was proving a trying and irritable tenant:

So far we are all civility with the Squire who was much pleased with my intention of remedying his grievances by a wall – but I find too much acquiescence will not do – the more is conceded the more is expected, and when one complaint is removed 2 or 3 others start up in its place – tis impossible to tranquillize a being whose only employ is to hunt out nuisances and whose greatest pleasure is to torment others by the narration of them –

After consultation with Mr Hailstone, her solicitor, and other advisers, Sarah herself settled on a suitable agent. The general opinion was that 'John Dixon the plaisterer was the best person to employ both to plan and effect the sale of the two small feilds for building – he has this morning measured them, but I must first promise them'.

John Dixon had not quite landed the big fish, however. Sarah Whittaker was at least as wily and reluctant to commit herself as he was anxious to acquire her land. The Townhill estate was not far from the centre of the developing town, its fields adjacent to Dead Lane (now Vicar Lane) and within a few hundred yards of the projected new Leeds road. He worked hard to convince her of his reliability and his proposals were carefully worked out. Sarah reported every word of Mr Dixon's remarks to her son:

> Cottages or at least small Houses are chiefly in request so near the town (for larger ones more distant situations are preferred) and to such our two small Feilds must be destined. By his calculations they are broad enough after completing Buck Street to admit two other streets – the last having a row of single houses with their backs and no windows to the Ing – a row at the bottom towards Boggart Lane and 2 or 3 larger building lots to face the Wakefield Road expected to fetch a higher price. Dixon calculates that averaging the whole at 6/- per yard the Feild woud produce upwards of £3000, and is of opinion that the sooner our intention of selling is made known, the better.

Sarah found Dixon's detailed ideas on the type of buildings to be erected distasteful, and yet she sensed that she was helpless to try and influence him. He knew what was required in these days of 'progress', and she felt old-fashioned and even reactionary in the face of modern ideas:

> Dixon is on Monday to draw me a plan of the streets and building lots which according to his present Ideas will be more like a Rabbit Warren than part of a Town – but such is the demand and we must swim with the

stream and make our advantage of it. Mr Pollard says we should make the most of Townhill by pulling it down and selling the materials and covering the Land with Houses – he means letting others do so.

But I hope in a year or two better Houses may be in request and the Rabbit Warren be excluded from my view by better Streets. The little Feilds seem likely to turn to excellent account and I hear from all hands a very good character of Dixon's honesty and sagacity. – he so well knows the wants and usages of the class of people he has to deal with –

Sarah impatiently awaited her son William's reply to this letter, for, as she said, 'we must be at a standstill until your letter arrives'. Although she was at least as sagacious as her son, Sarah was still inhibited from coming to any decision alone. Women always deferred to the senior male in the family.

William's view was that they should attempt to sell only

A view of Bradford from the south-east, around 1840, looking towards the town from the vicinity of Townhill.

leases and keep the freehold. Not unnaturally, John Dixon was unenthusiastic. Sarah reported again:

I consulted Dixon on your idea of selling only the Leasehold he says he would do so if we wished it, but it would be less advantageously, that is, we should get less in proportion, as those who have saved money to purchase a lot for a cottage wd rather buy the freehold or stipulate that they should do so as soon as they could raise the money –

In spite of the exhausting negotations with Dixon, Sarah had enjoyed the Bradford visit and seeing so many old friends:

I have been playing picquet with Miss Swaine – Sally went on Thursday to spend a few days at Gomersal and I shall take a ride to fetch her this afternoon – and tomorrow afternoon we must take leave of our Friends at Quarry Cottage – we had a letter from Lancaster lately – Mrs Sharpe has arrived there and as her furniture was taken into her new House, the late occupiers had a sale of their own in the yard, was not this abominable usage when she had accommodated them, staying a week or two more than the agreement – the post waits so a hasty adieu my Dr William, from your affectionate Mother S Whittaker.

This letter is the last we hear of Sarah Whittaker's voice. She retreated to her new house at Castle Hill, Lancaster, and spent the rest of her days quietly, living with her unmarried daughter.

In December 1824, William went to Bradford on his mother's behalf to collect her rents. 'I almost broke my neck on a hired horse in Thornton Road', he wrote. Mr Duffield, it seemed, was still resident at Townhill and Dixon, whom he had only seen for a moment, had not sold much more land than he had the previous August. Selling was proving rather slow after all the excitement.

In 1826 Mr Duffield is recorded as paying a half-yearly rent of £81 plus £1 2s 6d for fixtures, and £1 13s for 'wall', presumably the wall which had remedied his 'grievance'.

Sale particulars of the Townhill estate were prepared in 1831, by Joseph Smith, surveyor and land agent, on behalf of the Reverend William Whittaker. The layout of the mansion of Townhill with its outbuildings, shrubbery, courtyard and garden is indicated, and below the house, at the bottom of the Townhill field, is the huddle of houses and other buildings, which comprised the 'old house and premises' where Sarah spent many years of her life. The Ing (one of the estate fields) contained George Street, already 'formed into a street' which Sarah had disliked so much, and where she had stayed at Mrs Reed's house on her last visit to Bradford. Above it were the fields Whitelands and Little Whitelands. Across Boggart Lane were Sarah's other fields, Crosse Close and Penny Oak.

In 1837, Sarah Whittaker died, at the age of seventy-seven, leaving her letters as an intimate record of an eighteenth century business family's life and times. Naturally she could not bear to destroy them, and nor could any of her descendants. They found their way eventually into the archives of a library somewhere in the Bradford district, and from there to the Bradford archives.

Sarah lived through the American Revolution, the French Revolution, the Napoleonic Wars, the birth-pangs of the Industrial Revolution, and the reigns of three kings. She died in the year Queen Victoria came to the throne.

During her lifetime she had seen her home town change out of all recognition. It had grown from a peaceful, small, semi-rural manufacturing town into a dirty, smoky, immensely rich and immensely squalid industrial city, mushrooming with mill chimneys and packed with the insanitary dwellings of ill-paid millworkers. Dr John Simpson, the diarist, found Bradford in 1825 'an abominable manufacturing district. There is no kind of society here', he declared roundly. And although the centre of the town was spick and

225

span, said John James the Bradford historian, in 1837 it was 'the dirtiest town in England . . . Bradford may be described as an accumulation of mean streets, steep lanes and huge mills – intersected here and there by those odious patches of black, muddy waste ground, rooted up by pigs and strewn with oyster shells, cabbage stalks and such garbage as I have often noticed in other manufacturing towns.'

Half a century earlier, he averred, just as disdainfully, it had been 'a mere collection of huts' – scarcely a description with which the Bucks and their circle would have agreed.

Townhill, which had once stood proudly on the hill looking down across its pleasant fields to the small town in the valley, had also had its day. It was a monument to a superseded way of life, and it was in the way of 'progress'. It was finally swallowed up during further development of the city and the coming of the railway.

In a century of rapid industrialisation, Bradford became the world capital for the manufacture of worsted cloth and retained its importance till the 1920s, when there began a gradual decline in its textile fortunes which has lasted to the present day.

Now, in the 1990s, the lines of the green hills which Sarah knew are reappearing here and there, glimpsed between decaying and demolished mill buildings and the urban detritus of a large but post-industrial city. Except in the letters, however, there is scarcely a trace of Sarah Whittaker's vanished world.

Postscript

In 1837 Joseph Smith, the surveyor, drew a plan for 'a new street' from the Leeds road through the properties of three landowners, one of whom was the Reverend William Whittaker. By this time, houses had been built on Frederick Street, which was parallel with George Street.

In 1850, Thomas Dixon, land agent and surveyor, offered twenty-five lots of freehold land at Townhill, Bradford, with the house as lot 1, and all the rest of the estate sectioned in building lots and criss-crossed with planned streets. There was a choice of vacant lots on Adolphus Street, Ernest Street, and Augustus Street, bisected by Diamond Street and Graham Street. Boggart Lane is now christened Eastbrook Lane. 'Buck Street' does not appear on this plan, although a Buck Street was created well to the east of the Townhill fields, perhaps on another part of Sarah's land.

In 1859, William Buck, son of Sarah's brother John William Buck, sold his father's farms at Denholme to the Bradford Corporation for reservoirs.

In an 1861 map of Bradford, Townhill House, misnamed 'Townend House', is still marked as a forlorn island on a hill, a reminder of a forgotten age, but much of the land had been swallowed up by the passenger station, sidings and goods yard of the Great Northern Railway, later the LNER. This became known as the Adolphus Street station. By 1876, the house had finally disappeared, to be replaced by terraces of small houses. The name 'Townhill Street', marked on the 1850 plan just below the house, lasted to the 1930s.

Today, most of the area of the Townhill estate is covered

by the six lane Shipley-Airedale Road, Bradford's north-eastern bypass, which now descends the hill from the Wakefield Road. Fragments of George Street, Frederick Street, Diamond Street, Adolphus Street and Ernest Street still remained until 1990 on either side of this new highway, when the area was transformed into a business park. The 'Wakefield Road Gyratory', in modern highways parlance, is the large road intersection which lies just below the site of Townhill House. The house itself was level with Hall Lane.

C 1720

SAMUEL DAWSON   *m*   SARAH H[
(LEEDS)

1742		
MARTHA *m* FREEMAN FLOWER	**MARGARET** *m* **STEPHEN T[**	REV THOMAS FABER
(GAINSBOROUGH)	*(Aunt Todd)* *(Mr Todd)*	(CALVERLEY)
	d 1795 (LONDON)	

LIDIA
(MISS FLOWER)

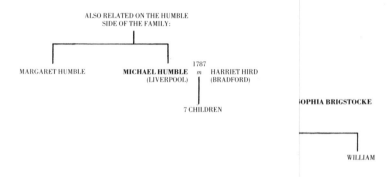

ALSO RELATED ON THE HUMBLE
SIDE OF THE FAMILY:

MARGARET HUMBLE   **MICHAEL HUMBLE**   *m*   HARRIET HIRD
(LIVERPOOL)   (BRADFORD)

1787

7 CHILDREN

₃OPHIA BRIGSTOCKE

WILLIAM

Table of Dates

229

		1789	George Washington first President of the United States
1791	Birth of William, son of Sarah and William Whittaker	1791–3	Negro revolt against French on island of Santo Domingo led by Toussaint L'Ouverture
1792	Birth of Sarah, daughter of Sarah and William Whittaker		
		1793	Outbreak of war between Britain and French Revolutionary government
		1793	Eli Whitney's invention of the cotton gin
1794	William Whittaker's bankruptcy		
1795	William's flight to America		
1796–9	William's voyages	1796	Spain joined France in war against Britain
		1801	Battle of Copenhagen
		1802	Peace of Amiens
		1803	War with France resumed
1804	William's return to England		
		1805	Battle of Trafalgar
1806	William's final voyage to America		
		1807	Britain abolished the slave trade

1810	Death of Caroline Buck		
		1811	The Prince of Wales appointed Prince Regent
1812	John William Buck's marriage to Sophia Brigstocke		
1814	Birth of John Buck		
1815	Death of infant John Buck	1815	The Battle of Waterloo
1816	Death of William Whittaker		
c1817	Sarah Whittaker's departure from Bradford		
		1820	Accession of George IV
1821	Death of John William Buck		
		1830	Accession of William IV
1837	Death of Sarah Whittaker	1837	Accession of Queen Victoria

Bibliography and Sources

Manuscript Sources

The Whittaker Papers.
The Hailstone Papers.
The Preston Papers.
The Diary of Abraham Balme 1775.
All the above are in the the West Yorkshire Archive, Bradford.

Printed Sources

Bradford

The Book of Bradford 1924. Hambley Rowe (ed). BMA.
Historical Notes on the Bradford Corporation. William Cudworth. 1881.
Musical Reminiscences of Bradford. William Cudworth.
Round About Bradford. William Cudworth.
Geography of Bradford. C Richardson. 1976.
Topographical Description of the County of York 1825. Cooke.
Black Dyke Mills. Eric Sigsworth.
The Genesis of the Industrial Revolution in Bradford 1760 to 1830. Dr Gary Firth.
Pen and Pencil Pictures of Old Bradford. William Scruton. 1891.
Bradford Fifty Years Ago. William Scruton. 1897
History of Bradford. John James. 1841 and 1866.
History of Bradford. J Fieldhouse. Bradford Libraries 1972.
The Diary of Dr John Simpson 1825. Bradford Libraries.
Bradford in History. Horace Hird. 1968.

Old Bradford Illustrated. Harry Fieldhouse. 1889.
Idlethorp. Wright Watson. 1951.
And the Glory - The History of the Huddersfield Choral Society. R A Edwards. Maney 1985.
Memorials of Calverley Church. Henry Stapleton.

Wakefield

Memories of Merry Wakefield. Henry Clarkson. Amethyst Press and Wakefield Historical Publications 1985.
Diaries of Mrs Anne Lumb of Silcoates. Charles Milnes Gaskell (ed). 1884.
Wakefield and its People. J W Walker.
Wakefield and Wool. John Goodchild. Wakefield Historical Publications 1981.
'Richmal Mangnall and her School at Crofton Hall'. Article by W G Briggs in *University of Leeds Institute of Education, Researches and Studies* No 15. 1957.

Liverpool

Liverpool As It Was. Richard Brooke. 1853.
Merchant Adventurers. G Chandler.
'The Port of Liverpool and the Crisis of 1793'. Article by Francis E Hyde Bradbury, B Parkinson and Sheila Mariner.
A General History of Liverpool. T Troughton. 1810.
History of Liverpool. James Wallace. 1797.

Manchester

Memorials of Manchester Streets. Sutcliffe. 1874.
Manchester Streets and Manchester Men. Swindells. 1907
Manchester: Its Political, Commercial and Social History. J Wheeler. 1836.
Manchester: A Short History. W H Shercliff. Manchester 1960.
Manchester of Yesterday. H G Stevens. John Sherratt & Son 1958.
Historical Sketches and Personal Recollections. Archibald Prentice 1851.
Origins of Manchester Street Names. Prentice.

The Strange Case of Thomas Walker. Frida Knight. Lawrence and Wishart 1957.

Manchester Merchants and Foreign Trade 1794-1858. Arthur Redford. Manchester University Press 1934.

The Rise and Fall of King Cotton. Anthony Burton. André Deutsch 1984.

Manchester Banks and Bankers. Leo Grindon. 1877.

A Picture of Manchester. Joseph Aston. 1816.

English Merchants. H R Fox-Bourne.

Salford, A City and Its Past. Tom Bergin, Dorothy N Pearce, Stanley Shaw (eds). Salford Council 1974.

Salford Through The Ages. Charles P Hampson. Salford City Reporter 1930.

Charleston, USA

Charleston: Crossroads of History. Isabella G Leland. South Carolina Historical Society.

South Carolina As Seen By A Famous Botanist. François André Michaux. *A Travelling Governor's View 1802*. John Drayton. Extracts reprinted in *South Carolina, The Grand Tour 1780-1865*. Thomas D Clark (ed). University of South Carolina Press 1973.

'The Letters of Charles Caleb Cotton 1798-1802'. *South Carolina Historical and Genealogical Magazine* July 1950 (Vol L11, No 3). Contributed by Julien Dwight Martin.

The Old Merchant Marine. South Carolina Historical Society.

Privateers in Charleston, 1793-1796. Jackson. Smithsonian Studies in History and Technology.

'Stranger's Fever'. M Foster Farley. Article in *South Carolina History Illustrated* Feb 1970.

'South Carolina War Hawks'. M Foster Farley. Article in *South Carolina History Illustrated* Aug 1970.

Charleston's Commercial Landscape, 1803-1860. Jeanne A Calhoun and Martha A Zierden. South Carolina Historical Society.

General

A Six Months Tour Through the North of England. Arthur Young. 1771.

English Social History. G M Trevelyan. Longmans 1944.

The Social History of English Music. E D Mackerness. Routledge and Kegan Paul 1964.

Sketch of a Tour into Derbyshire and Yorkshire. William Bray. 1777.

Description of the Country From Thirty to Forty Miles Round Manchester. J Aikin. 1795.

Children's Costume in England. Phillis Cunnington and Anne Buck. A & C Black.

The Defence of British Trade 1689-1815. Patrick Crowhurst. Dawson 1977.

The Growth of the British Cotton Trade 1780-1815. Michael M Edwards. Manchester University Press 1967.

The Trade Winds. A Study of British Overseas Trade During The French Wars 1793-1815. C N Parkinson (ed). Allen and Unwin 1948.